Tipbook Violin and Viola

The Complete Guide

Hugo Pinksterboer

Tipbook Violin and Viola

The Complete Guide

The Complete Guide to Your Instrument!

First edition published in 2001 by
The Tipbook Company bv, The Netherlands
Third edition published in 2008 by
Hal Leonard Books
An Imprint of Hal Leonard Corporation
7777 West Bluemound Road
Milwaukee, WI 53213

Trade Book Division Editorial Offices
19 West 21st Street, New York, NY 10010

Printed in the United States of America

Book design by Gijs Bierenbroodspot

Library of Congress Cataloging-in-Publication Data

Pinksterboer, Hugo.
Tipbook violin and viola : the complete guide / Hugo Pinksterboer. -- 3rd ed.
p. cm.
"The complete guide to your instrument."
Includes bibliographical references and index.
ISBN 978-1-4234-4276-9 (pbk.)
1. Violin. 2. Viola. I. Title.
ML750.P56 2008
787.2--dc22

2008041083

www.halleonard.com

Thanks!

For their information, their expertise, their time, and their help we'd like to thank the following musicians, teachers, technicians, and other violin experts:

Isabelle van Keulen, Nello Mirando, Theo Olof, Edward C. Campbell (violin maker, PA), David Rivinus (violin maker, OR), Duane Lightner (Discount String Center, IN), Kim Rodney and Frederik Habel (GEWA, Germany), Lang Shen (Knilling String Instruments, MO), Heinz Kovacs (Thomastik-Infeld, Austria), Sandy Neill (D'Addario, NY), Volker Müller-Zierach (Pirastro, Germany), Klaus Clement (Höfner, Germany), Barbara Van Itallie (Violin Society of America), Jacqueline and Serge Stam (violin makers), Michaël and Ina van Berkum (violin makers), Ulrike Wiebel (violinmaker), Levent Aslan, Mies Albarda (European String Teachers Association (ESTA/ ARCO), Jaap Bolink (violin maker), Taner Erkek, Harm van der Geest, Hilka Jelsma, Siard de Jong, Fred Lindeman (violin maker), Hans and Sonja Neuburger, Annelies Steinhauer (violin maker), Eduard van Tongeren (violin maker), Tom van Berkel, Bas van den Broek, Guust François (violin maker), Andreas Grütter (bow maker), Eric Matser, A.L. Matser, Marja Mosk, the late Fred Pinksterboer, Irmela Schlingensiepen (violin maker), Helena and Jelle van Tongeren, and Harry Vogel. The violin on the cover is played by Bregje van Tongeren.

About the Author

Journalist, writer, and musician **Hugo Pinksterboer**, author of The Tipbook Series, has published hundreds of interviews, articles, and reviews for national and international music magazines.

About the Designer

Illustrator, designer, and musician **Gijs Bierenbroodspot** has worked as an art director for a wide variety of magazines and has developed numerous ad campaigns. While searching in vain for information about saxophone mouthpieces, he got the idea for this series of books on music and musical instruments. He is responsible for the layout and illustrations for all of the Tipbooks.

Acknowledgments

Cover photo: René Vervloet and Gijs Bierenbroodspot
Editors: Robert L. Doerschuk, Michael J. Collins, and Meg Clark
Proofreaders: Nancy Bishop and Patricia Waddy

Anything missing?

Any omissions? Any areas that could be improved? Please go to www.tipbook.com to contact us, or send an email to info@tipbook.com. Thanks!

Contents

Introduction

Are you thinking about buying a violin or a viola, or do you want to learn more about the instrument you already have? If so, this book will tell you everything you need to know. You'll learn about auditioning violins and bows, selecting strings, and maintaining and tuning your instrument, and there's information on the history, the family, and the making of the violin – and much, much more.

Having read this Tipbook, you'll be able to get the most out of your instrument, to buy the best violin or viola you can, and to easily grasp any other literature on the subject, from books and magazines to online publications.

The first four chapters

If you have just started playing, or haven't yet begun, pay particular attention to the first four chapters. They explain the basics of the violin, the viola, and the bow, and inform you on learning to play the instrument, practicing, and buying or renting an instrument. This information also fully prepares you to read the rest of the book.

Advanced players

Advanced players can skip ahead to Chapter 5, where you find everything you need to know to make an informed choice when you're going to buy or rent a violin or a viola. Chapters 6 and 7 offer similar information on selecting strings, a bow, and rosin.

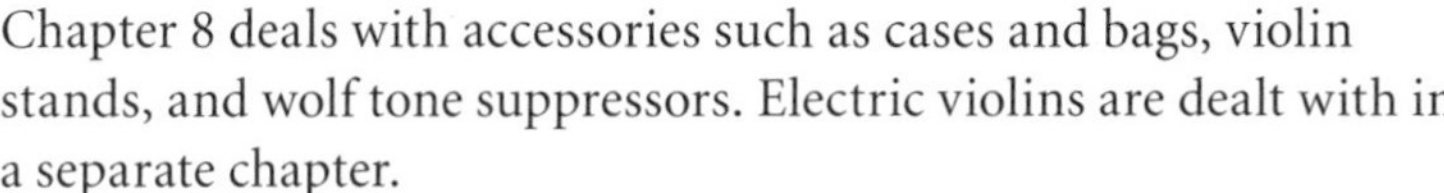

Chapter 8 deals with accessories such as cases and bags, violin stands, and wolf tone suppressors. Electric violins are dealt with in a separate chapter.

Tuning and maintenance

Chapters 10 and 11 help you get the best out of your instrument by offering helpful information on tuning and maintaining your precious violin or viola.

Background information

The final chapters offer essential reading material on the history of the violin, the family of the instrument, the way it is made, and on its makers.

US dollars

Please note that all price indications listed on the following pages are based on estimated street prices in US dollars.

Glossary

The glossary at the end of the book briefly explains most of the terms you'll come across as a string player. Also included are an index of terms, and a couple of pages for essential notes on your equipment.

Practicing

As an extra, this edition of *Tipbook Violin and Viola* provides you with a general chapter on effective practicing. Enjoy.

– Hugo Pinksterboer

See and Hear What You Read with Tipcodes

www.tipbook.com

In addition to the many illustrations on the following pages, Tipbooks offer you a new way to see – and even hear – what you are reading about. The Tipcodes that you will come across throughout this book give you access to short videos, sound files, and other additional information at www.tipbook.com.

How it works is very simple. One example: On page 53 of this book you can read about using fine tuners. Below that paragraph there is a short section marked **Tipcode VIOLIN-006**. Type in that code on the Tipcode page at www.tipbook.com and you will see a short movie that shows you how to use them.

Tipcode VIOLIN-006
This short video demonstrates the use of a fine tuner.

Enter code, watch movie

You enter the Tipcode below the movie window on the Tipcode

page. In most cases, you will then see the relevant images within five to ten seconds. Tipcodes activate a short movie, sound, or both, or a series of photos.

Tipcode list

For your convenience, the Tipcodes presented in this book are also listed on page 212.

Quick start

The Tipcode movies, photo series, and soundtracks are designed so that they start quickly. If you miss something the first time, you can of course repeat them. And if it all happens too fast, use the pause button below the movie window.

First, make your selection: Tipcode, chords and fingering charts, or the glossary.

The Tipcode window displays videos, fingering charts, chords, or a glossary of the terms used in this book.

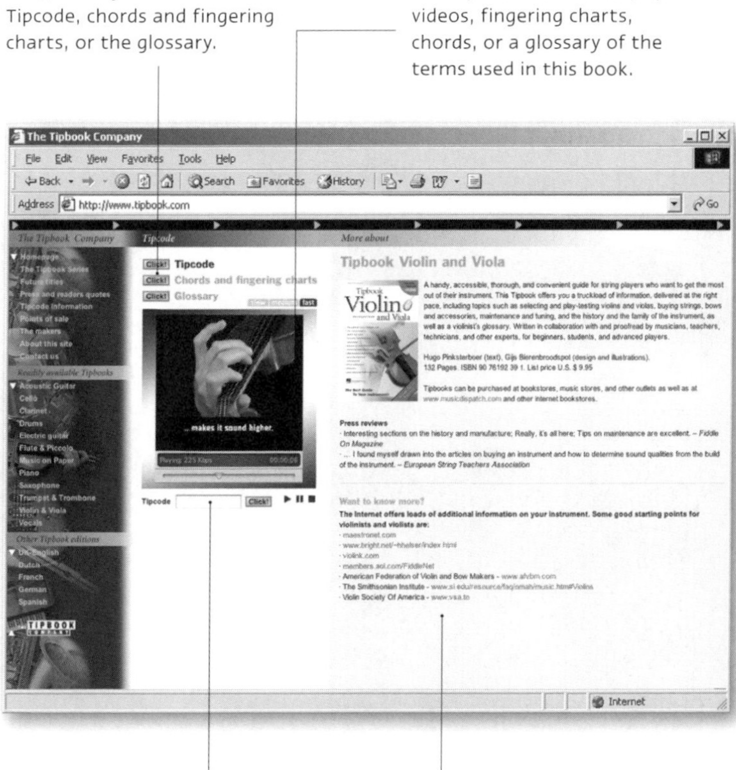

These links take you directly to other interesting sites.

These links take you directly to other interesting sites.

Plug-ins

If the software you need to view the videos is not yet installed on your computer, you'll automatically be told which software you need, and where you can download it. This software is free. Questions? Check out 'About this site' at www.tipbook.com.

Still more at www.tipbook.com

You can find even more information at www.tipbook.com. For instance, you can look up words in the glossaries of all the Tipbooks published to date. There are chord diagrams for guitarists and pianists; fingering charts for saxophonists, clarinetists, and flutists; and rudiments for drummers. Also included are links to most of the websites mentioned in the *Want to Know More?* section of each Tipbook.

1

Violinists and Violists

Practicing the violin is something you usually do by yourself. Performing, on the other hand, you'll usually do with others. In an orchestra, with twenty or thirty other violinists, or in a string quartet with two violins, a viola, and a cello. Or in a band, perhaps playing jazz, rock, or folk music. A chapter on the world of the violin, and on what makes it such a great instrument.

Violins and violas are *string instruments.* You play them by drawing a bow across the strings. That's why they're also known as *bowed instruments.*

Bigger and lower

The viola looks just the same as the violin. The main difference is that the viola is a little bigger. As a result, it sounds a little lower.

Tipcode VIOLIN-001
This Tipcode demonstrates the difference between a violin and a viola, playing a scale on both instruments.

All kinds of styles

Most violinists play classical music, but you'll find them in many other styles too — in folk music from different countries, in gypsy music and Jewish klezmer, in tango and Turkish music, but also in the blues, Cajun, country, rock, and jazz.

Tipcode VIOLIN-002
The violin can be used in a wide variety of styles, as you can hear in this Tipcode.

Classical

There is a wide variety of classical violin music available. That's

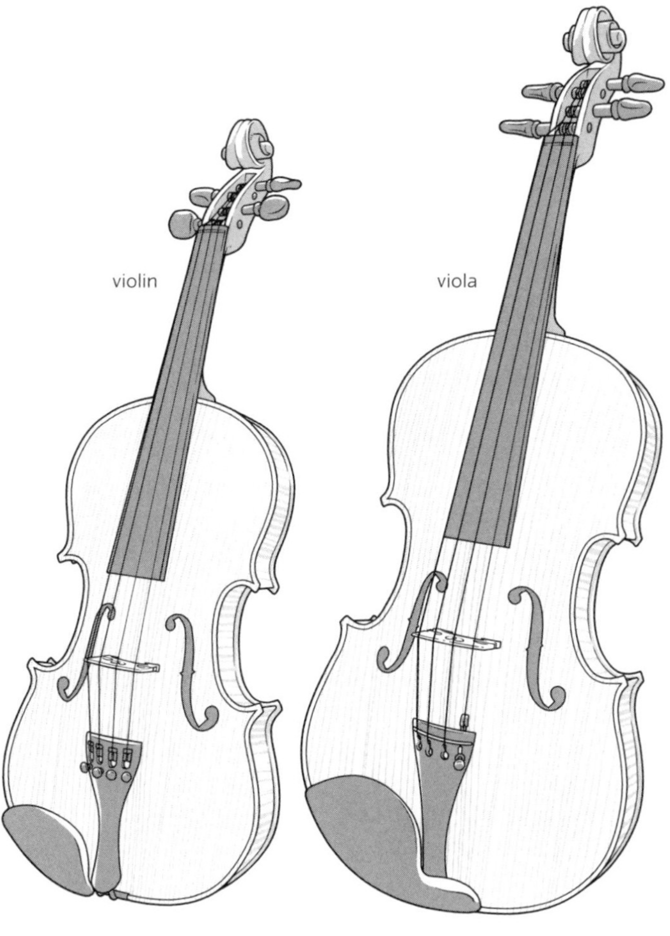

A viola is slightly bigger than a violin.

not surprising, because the instrument has been around for some four centuries. All in all there is so much violin music that you couldn't play it in a lifetime.

Small and large

Classical music can be played in large and small orchestras, in quartets, and in many other kinds of groups and ensembles. Here are some examples.

Symphony orchestra

The violin is the main voice of the largest orchestra of all, the symphony orchestra, with some fifty to a hundred or more members. Besides the violin and the viola, a symphony orchestra includes two other, larger string instruments: the *cello*, which stands between the legs of the cellist; and the *double bass*, the largest of them all.

Other instruments

Besides these four types of bowed instruments (violin, viola, cello, double bass) you'll find all kinds of other instruments in the symphony orchestra, such as:

- brasswinds (trumpet, French horn, trombone, etcetera);
- woodwinds (clarinet, flute, oboe, bassoon, and so on);
- percussion instruments (snare drums, tympani, cymbals, etcetera);
- a harp, a grand piano...

More than thirty

Violins aren't very loud, but they're very important to the sound of a symphony orchestra. That's why there are more of them than any other instrument. A typical orchestra may have sixteen violinists, and some have more than thirty.

First and second violins

The violinists are always divided into two groups: the first and second violinists. You could think of the first violinists as the singer

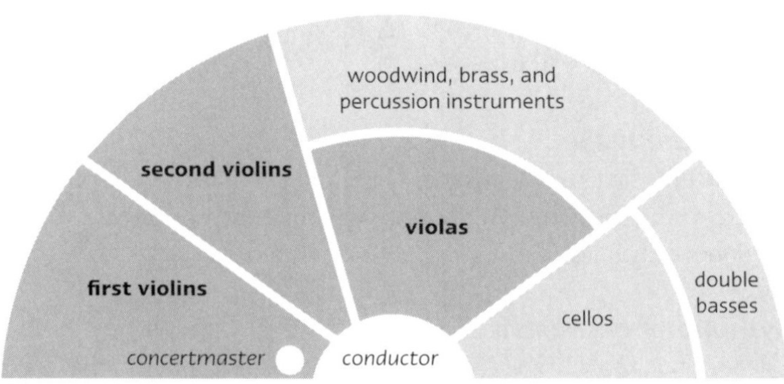

An example of the arrangement of the instruments in a symphony orchestra. The violins are always at the front.

of the band: They often play the melody that you go on humming to yourself after a concert. The second violinists, who are equally important, usually accompany the melody.

The violists

The viola players, also known as *violists*, have their own role. The different string sections are not unlike the different groups of singers in a choir. A large orchestra may have sixteen violists.

Concertmasters

The strings are always at the front, around the conductor. To the conductor's left, right at the front, is the *concertmaster*, who is the leader of all the musicians in the orchestra. The second violins and the violas each have their own leaders as well; they're the principal second violinist and the principal violist. The louder instruments, such as the trumpets and percussion instruments, are further toward the back.

String quartet

A lot of classical music has been written for smaller groups too. A well-known and very popular ensemble is the *string quartet*, for instance, with two violinists, a violist and a cellist.

A few bars from a string quartet (W. A. Mozart); music for two violins, viola, and cello.

Duo and solo

There is also a lot of music for duos — a violinist and a pianist, for example. There are even pieces that are meant to be played solo — just a violin, and nothing else. Of course, that's a different type of solo playing than when you play 'solo' violin accompanied by a full orchestra.

Violin or viola?

Many violists started out on a violin — only later did they discover that they preferred the lower, warmer sound of a viola. Of course, you can also start on a viola. If you make the switch later, the viola will take a bit of getting used to.

2

A Quick Tour

A violin has a body, a neck and a fingerboard, four strings, four pegs, and a whole list of other parts. A chapter about what everything's called, what it's for and where to find it, about the differences between violins and violas, and about violins for children.

The violin you see on the next page looks remarkably like a violin made a hundred or more years ago.

Viola

A viola is slightly bigger, which makes it sound lower and a bit darker. That's the main difference between the two.

Children

Violins and violas made specially for children's hands are also available (see page 18).

Body

The main part of the violin, the *body*, is the soundbox of the instrument. It amplifies the sound of the strings.

Top and back

The *top* and the *back* of the body are noticeably arched. The top, with two *f*-shaped *soundholes* or *f-holes*, is most important for the sound of the instrument.

Tuning pegs

You tune the strings using the pegs or tuning pegs. There is one peg for each string, at the top of the violin. The pegs are fitted in the pegbox.

Scroll

The head of the instrument is known as the scroll, with the spiral-shaped volute on top of it. On some violins, this section is shaped like a lion's head or an angel, for example.

Fingerboard

The strings run along the fingerboard. To make the strings produce higher notes, you stop them by pressing them onto the fingerboard. Stopping a string makes the section that vibrates shorter. As a result, the string will produce a higher tone.

The neck

The fingerboard is a thin, dark plank that's glued to the neck. The neck runs from the scroll to the body. The fingerboard is quite a

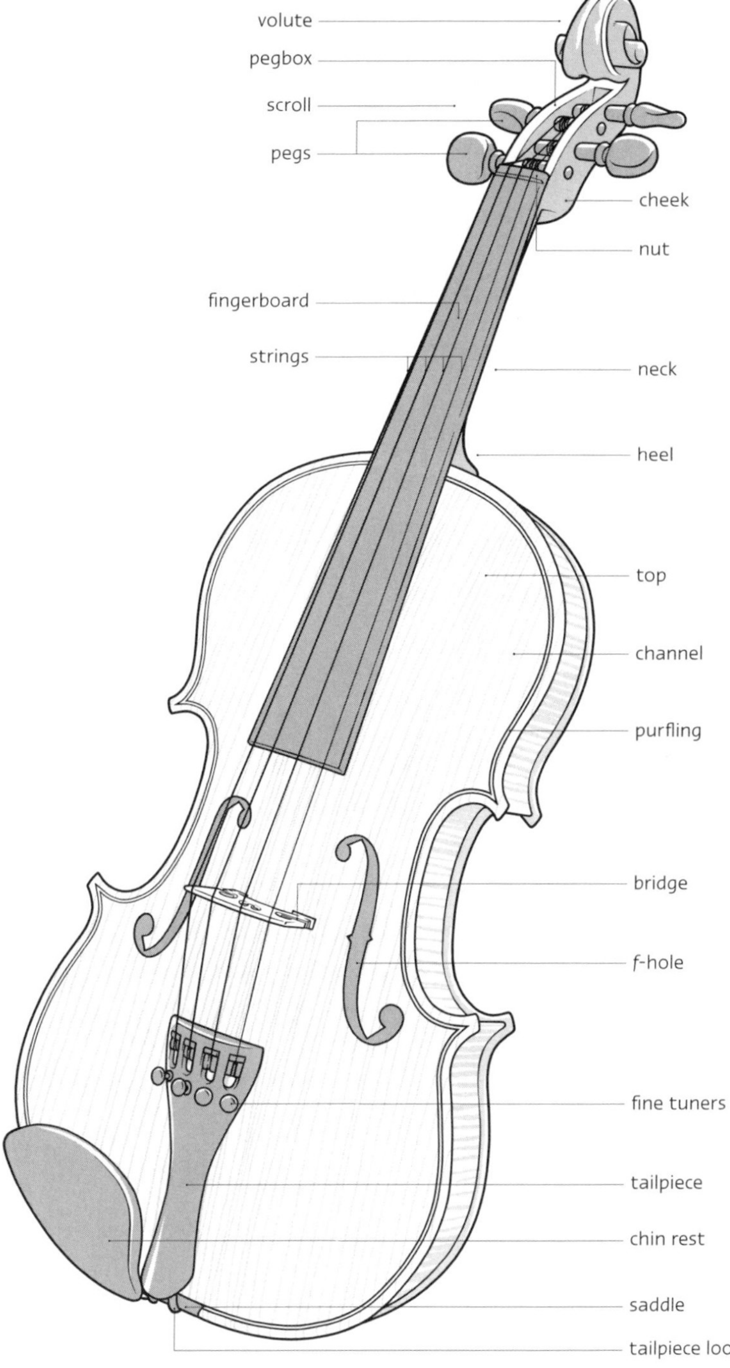
volute
pegbox
scroll
pegs
cheek
nut
fingerboard
strings
neck
heel
top
channel
purfling
bridge
f-hole
fine tuners
tailpiece
chin rest
saddle
tailpiece loop

Tipcode VIOLIN-003
This Tipcode demonstrates how stopping a string makes it produce a higher pitch.

bit longer than the neck: A considerable section juts out over the body.

Nut

At the top end of the fingerboard, where the it meets the scroll, the strings run over a small ridge called the *nut*.

The bridge

About halfway down the body, the strings run over the bridge, a flat piece of wood that's much lighter in color than the rest of the violin. The shape of the bridge tells you where its name comes from.

The strings, the bridge, and the top

When you play, you're actually making the strings vibrate with your bow. The bridge passes on those vibrations to the top. This makes sure the instrument will be heard. The top, together with the rest of the body, amplifies the sound of the strings.

Rounded bridge

The bridge is rounded, just like the top of the fingerboard. This allows you to bow the two middle strings without touching the outer ones.

Feet

The bridge stands on the top on its two feet, without the help of glue or screws. The pressure of the strings is enough to make sure it doesn't fall over.

Tailpiece and fine tuners

The strings are attached to the pegs at one end, and to the *tailpiece* at the other. Inside the tailpiece there are usually one or more *fine tuners*. These small, metal tuning machines make tuning your instrument a lot easier.

Tailpiece loop, end button, and saddle

The tailpiece is attached to the (*end*) *button* with a loop known as the *tailpiece loop*. To make sure this loop doesn't damage the body, it runs over the *saddle* or *bottom nut*.

Chin rest

When you play the violin, you chin will be in the instrument's *chin rest*. These chin rests come in many different shapes and sizes.

Shoulder rest

The back of the violin rests on your shoulder. A *shoulder rest* — or a small pillow — makes it sit a little higher. Even so, violinists and

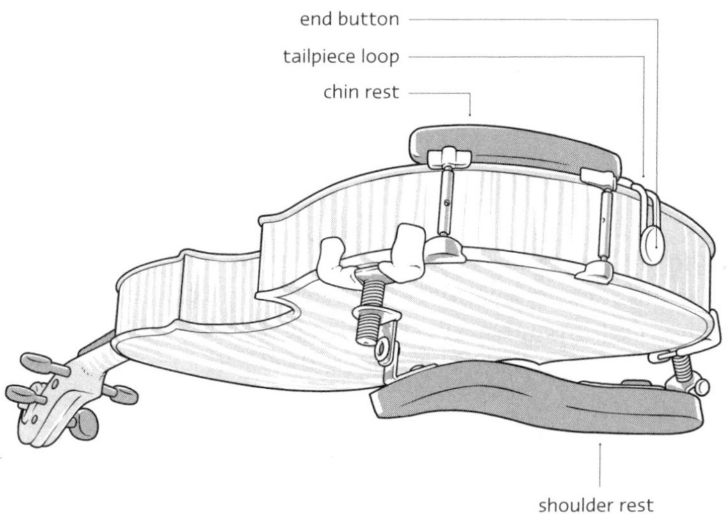

violists need to tilt their heads to the left a little while playing.

Fittings

The shoulder rest, chin rest, tailpiece, pegs, and end button are collectively known as the *fittings* or the *trim* of the instrument.

Purfling

The inlaid *purfling* runs along the edge of the body. It is usually made of three strips of wood — two ebony or dark dyed strips, and a lighter wood in between.

Channel

From the edge, the top usually dips a little, before the upward arching begins. This 'valley' is called the *channel.* The back has almost the same shape as the top.

Heel and shoulder

The semicircular part that sticks out at the top of the back is called the *heel.* The shoulder, the wider bottom part of the neck that links it to the body, is glued to that heel.

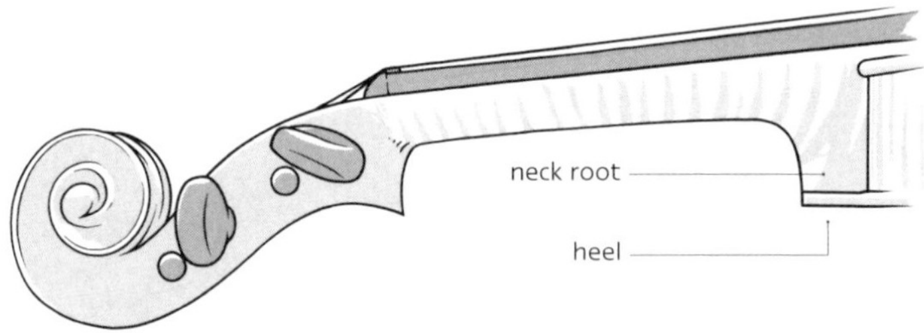

Violin or viola?

Violas are not only a bit wider and taller than violins, but they're slightly deeper too. The sides of the body (the *ribs*) are higher. A detail: Some violas have a kind of 'step' near the pegbox.

Lower and darker

As a result of its larger dimensions, a viola sounds not only lower, but also a bit darker and fuller than a violin. That difference in timbre is larger than what the difference in pitch alone would suggest. (Lower tones tend to sound darker than higher ones.)

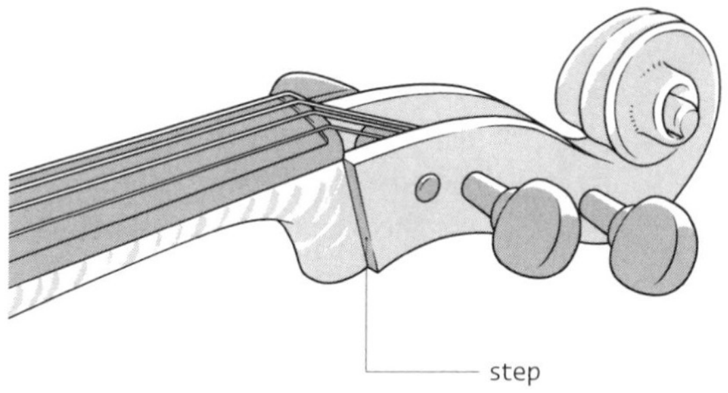

You can sometimes tell a viola by this 'step.'

INSIDE

There is plenty to see inside a violin too, from the sound post to the bass bar, the maker's label, and a number of small wooden blocks.

The sound post

If you look through the *f*-hole at the *treble side* of the instrument (by the thinnest string), you can just about see a small wooden

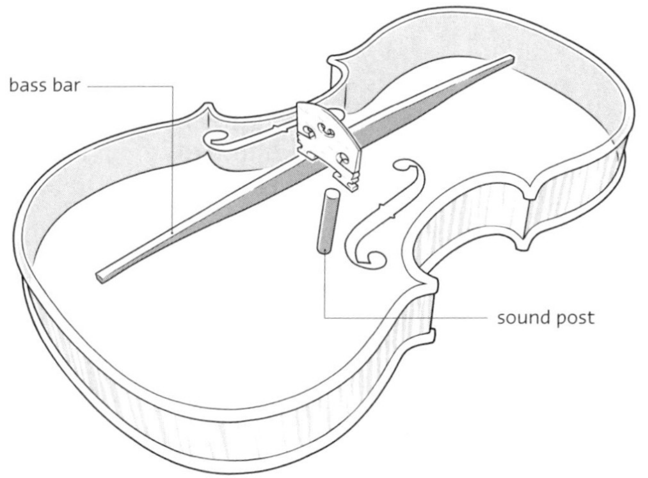

The bass bar and sound post are important to the sound of a violin.

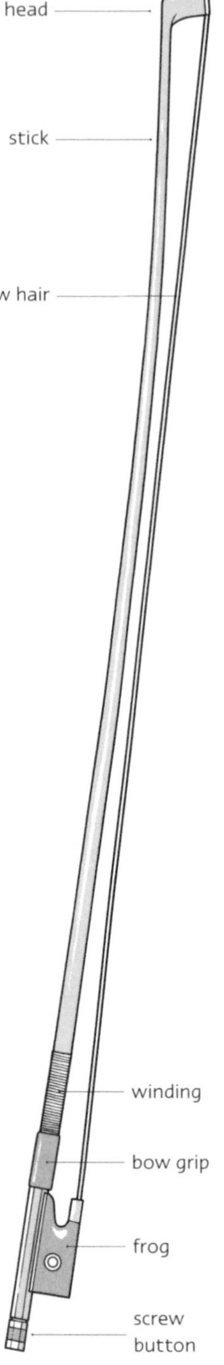

rod, wedged between the top and the back. That's the *sound post.* Without it, a violin would sound very thin or hollow.

The bass bar

Near the other *f*-hole, on the *bass side*, is the *bass bar.* This wooden bar strengthens the top and enhances the lower frequencies of the instrument.

The label

You'll be able to see only a tiny bit of the bass bar, by looking from the side and through the top part of the *f*-hole. If you look straight down through the same hole, you may see the violin maker's label.

THE BOW

Your violin bow is almost as important as the instrument itself.

Bow hair and stick

The bow hair — some hundred and fifty hairs — almost always comes from a horse's tail. One end of the hair is held in place inside the *head* or *tip*, at the top end of the *stick* or *bow stick*. The other end is held in place inside the *frog.*

Bow grip

You hold the bow at the (*bow*) *grip* and the *winding.* The bow grip is typically made of leather. The thin, metal wire of the winding enhances your grip and helps protect the wood.

Tension

Before you play, you have to tension the bow hair. Turn the screw button clockwise until there's about 0.25" (5–6 mm) between the hair and the middle of the stick. When you're done playing, turn the screw button counterclockwise until the hair goes slack. The screw button is also known as **end screw** ***or*** **adjuster.**

Rosin

For the bow to do its job properly, you need to rub the hair with a piece of violin *rosin*. This makes the hair slightly sticky. Without rosin, the bow will slide across the strings without producing a sound.

STRINGS AND CLEFS

Both the violin and the viola have four strings, which come in steel, gut or synthetic versions. The thicker strings are usually wound with ultra-thin metal wire.

Violin: G, D, A, E

The four violin strings are tuned to the notes G, D, A, and E, as shown on the piano keyboard on page 17. The G is the lowest sounding string; the thin E the highest.

Viola: C, G, D, A

The illustration below also shows the notes of the viola strings. The thickest, lowest sounding string produces a C. The other three viola strings are tuned to the same pitches as the three lowest violin strings: G, D, and A.

Violin music on paper

Violin music is written in a staff that begins with the *G clef*, also known as the *treble clef.* The tail of this curly symbol circles the second line from below, indicating the note G. This G (G4) sounds an octave higher than the lowest note you can play on a violin (G3).

Treble clef

In some languages, the treble clef is known as the violin clef!

The viola key

When using the G clef, the lowest note of a viola (the C) requires no less than four ledger lines. This would make these low notes very hard to read. That's why viola music is written in a different clef: the *C clef.* Both the C clef and the F clef are shown on page 5.

A4

The A-string of a violin sounds the same pitch as the A to the right of Middle C on a piano keyboard. This A is known as A4 (or a', in

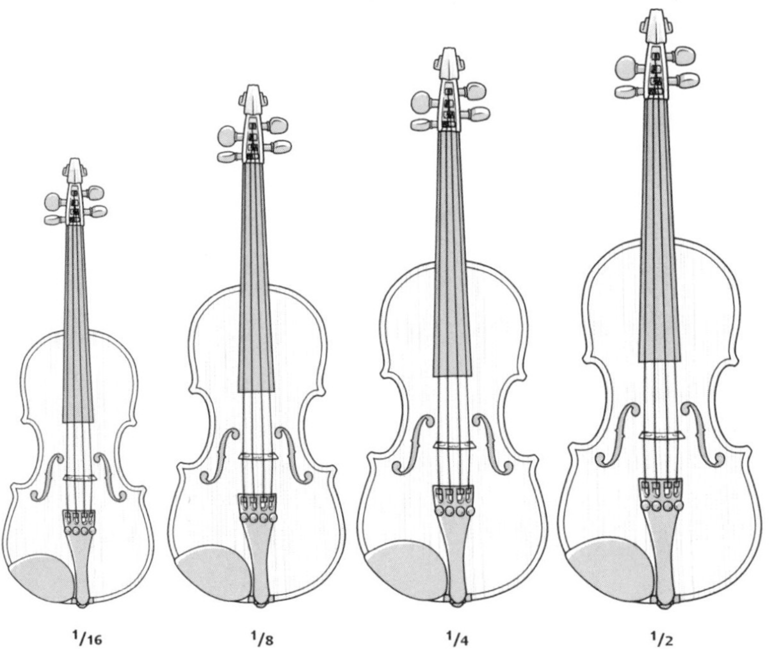

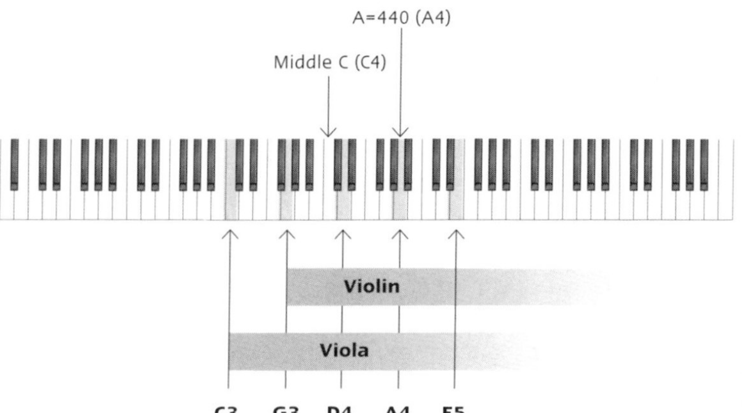

some countries). It is also the pitch to which most musicians tune their instruments. The exact pitches of the other strings are indicated in the illustration above.

CHILDREN'S INSTRUMENTS

A full-size violin is too big for most children under twelve. That's why there are violins in small or *fractional* sizes. Violas come in fractional sizes too.

Violin sizes

An 'adult' violin is usually referred to as a *full-size violin.* On paper this is shown as 4/4. Contrary to what the term suggests, a half-size (1/2) violin is just slightly smaller than a 4/4. The illustrations on the previous two pages show the most common violin sizes.

Viola sizes

Viola sizes are expressed in inches, referring to the length of the body of the instrument. Adults typically play a 16" or 16.5" viola. A 12" viola is about as big as a 1/2 violin.

A half or a quarter

There is no absolute rule for which size goes with which age. One seven-year-old might be better off with a 1/4 violin, while another child of that age needs a half-size. That's why you always need to try the instrument for size. The same goes for the bow. A teacher will know how to find the right size instrument for your child, and so will a good salesperson or a violin maker. Tip: *It's not only the child's finger and arm lengths that count; finger strength and other factors come into play as well.*

String length

Violins also differ in *string length* or *scale*, i.e., the distance from the nut to the bridge. For example, a 1/2 violin with a relatively large string length may be the right choice for a 'half-size' violinist with fairly big hands. There's more on this subject on pages 41–42 and 210 (String length).

3

Learning to Play

The violin may not be the easiest instrument to get started on, but it won't take years before you can perform on it. A chapter about learning to play, lessons, and practicing.

When you just start out, you need to get used to the feeling of having an instrument between your chin and your shoulder. Also, your left hand may initially feel like it's bent at an odd angle — and bowing the strings isn't easy either, at first.

Pizzicato

You can also play the violin by plucking the strings with your fingers. This is known as *pizzicato*. Many teachers start their pupils off with this technique to get them accustomed to using the left hand.

Tipcode VIOLIN-004

Play this Tipcode to see a violinist plucking the strings: pizzicato!

No markers

To play the violin in tune, you have to put your fingers in exactly the right places on the fingerboard. This too takes time to learn, as a violin's fingerboard has no markers or frets, like a guitar.

Techniques

Over the years, teachers have developed various techniques to

Finding the exact place...

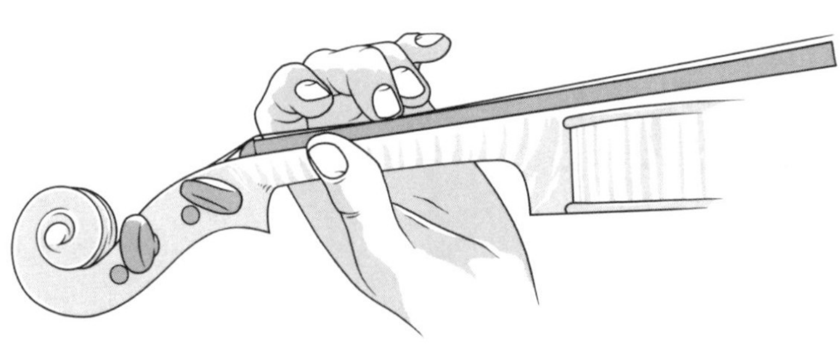

make learning the violin less hard than it may sound here — and there are thousands of very young violinists to demonstrate that it can be done. Many kids start playing the instrument at ages three or four.

LESSONS

If you take violin lessons, you'll learn about everything connected with playing the instrument — from bowing technique and reading music to a good posture.

Finding a teacher

Are your looking for a private teacher? Violin makers and dealers may be able to refer you to a violin or viola teacher, and music stores may have teachers on staff. You can also consult your local Musicians' Union or the orchestra teacher at a high school in your vicinity, or check the classified ads in newspapers and in music magazines.

Teachers can also be found online (see page 216 for some starting points), and some players have found great teachers in musicians they have seen in performance.

Prices

Professional private teachers will usually charge between twenty-five and seventy-five dollars per hour. Some make house calls, for which you'll pay extra.

Collectives

You also may want to check whether there are any teacher collectives or music schools in your vicinity. These collectives and schools typically offer all kinds of extras such as ensemble playing, master classes, and clinics, in a wide variety of styles, and at various levels.

Group or individual lessons

Instead of taking individual lessons, you can also go for group lessons if that's an option in your vicinity. Private lessons are more expensive, but they can be tailored exactly to your needs.

Questions, questions

On your first visit to a teacher, don't simply ask how much it costs. Here are some other questions.

- Is an **introductory lesson** included? This is a good way to find out how well you get on with the teacher, and, for that matter, with the instrument.
- Is the teacher interested in taking you on as a student if you are just doing it **for the fun of it**, or are you expected to practice at least three hours a day?
- Do you have to make a large investment in **method books** right away, or is course material provided?
- Can you **record your lessons**, so that you can listen at home to how you sound, and once more to what's been said?
- Is this teacher going to make you **practice scales** for two years, or will you be pushed onto a stage as soon as possible?

Non-classical

Because violinists mainly play classical music, most violin teachers give 'classical' lessons. Of course, some teachers are equally at home in other musical styles, if not more so. So if you want to play jazz violin, you will probably be able to find yourself a jazz violin teacher. That said, you can always benefit from what 'classical' teachers have to offer too, regardless of your own style.

More information

For more information on assessing a teacher and all related subjects, please consult Tipbook Music for Kids and Teens, a Guide for Parents *(see page 223).*

PRACTICE

You can play without learning to read music — even the violin — and you can learn to play without a teacher. But there's no substitute for practice, as you will read in Chapter 16. First, here are some practical tips for violin practicing.

A practice mute

Violins don't make a lot of noise, but they are loud enough to bother other people when you are practicing. There are various ways to overcome this. First of all, you can buy a *practice mute*, available in wood, metal, and rubber, for some five to fifteen dollars. You simply slide this short, thick 'comb' onto the bridge of your violin, where it effectively mutes most of the sound you produce — so it's best not to use one if your working on your tone. Other types of mutes are covered in Chapter 8.

Tipcode VIOLIN-005

A practice mute effectively reduces the instrument's volume, as you can hear in this Tipcode.

Tissue

If you lay a paper tissue over the body, covering the *f*-holes, the sound will become a little softer still. What's more, the rosin which comes off the bow when you play won't land on your violin, which saves on cleaning. You can use a practice mute to fix the tissue to the bridge.

Electric violin

Another, much more expensive solution would be to buy an electric violin. Some of these instruments have been specifically designed for silent practicing. You play them using a pair of headphones. The extremely modest sound of the strings is amplified by a small built-in amp. There's more on electric violins in Chapter 9.

Silent Violin (Yamaha)

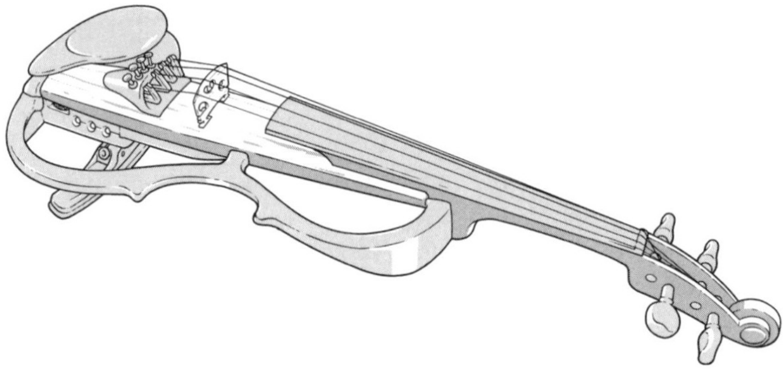

Practice violins

Practice violins or *mute violins* have become very rare: They're violins without a soundbox, basically, so nobody hears you playing — but you don't hear yourself either. This makes it unsuitable for working on your intonation or timbre, for instance.

Someplace else

It's always best to practice an acoustic instrument without mufflers, mutes, or other sound-reducing accessories. So if sound really is a problem, consider finding a formal practice space someplace else. For example, schools and music schools may have practice cubicles that you can use.

More on practicing

Chapter 16 in this book tells you more about making practicing fun and effective, with information on using your computer, tips on recording your practice sessions, and the use of metronomes.

Listen and play

Learning to play the instrument is not only about practicing;

it's also about listening to music. So visit festivals, concerts, and other performances. Go listen to orchestras, string quartets, and other ensembles. One of the best ways to learn to play is seeing other musicians at work. Living legends or local amateurs — every concert's a learning experience. And the best way to learn to play? Play a lot!

4

Buying or Renting?

Violin prices range from a few hundred to a few million dollars... A guide to violin prices, and to buying or renting an instrument.

Children under twelve often start off on a rented instrument, which can be exchanged for a larger size after you've grown a bit. Even if you are well beyond that age, renting a violin or viola can be a good way to start. It allows you to find out either if you like playing the instrument at all, or if you like a specific instrument.

Rental fees

Rental fees are usually set as a percentage of the retail price of the instrument. You can rent a full-sized student *outfit* (violin, bow, and case) from around fifteen dollars a month. Fractional-sized instruments are not always cheaper to rent. Usually, there's a minimum rental period — three months, for instance, or a school year.

The basics

It is impossible to provide a detailed description of the infinite amount of different plans, terms, and conditions you will likely encounter when you decide to rent an instrument. But here are the basics:

- Many rental plans are actually **rent-to-own plans**: The instrument is yours once the periodic payments you've made equal the list price. Note that this list price will usually be higher than what you would have paid had you just bought the instrument outright — which explains why most of these plans are interest free.
- Most of these rent-to-own or **hire-purchase plans** also have an option to buy the instrument before you're fully paid up; if you choose to buy the instrument, your rent paid to date will usually be applied to the instrument.
- With a lease plan — also known as a straight rental plan or **rent-to-rent plan** — you simply keep paying rent until you return the instrument. Rates are usually lower on these plans than those of rent-to-own plans. With these plans, renting for a long period of time will be, of course, more expensive than buying the instrument.

Maintenance and insurance

Maintenance is usually included in the rental fee, but some plans

offer it as a separate expense. The main thing is to make sure you don't have to worry about it. Insurance may be included as well. Make sure you understand what is and isn't covered under your lease or rental plan.

- Does the fee **include** instrument set-up, maintenance, and finance or bank charges?
- If **insurance** is included, does it also cover theft and loss?
- Do you get a **replacement** instrument if yours needs maintenance?
- Do you have to pay an origination fee, an application fee, or a deposit? These **fees** are usually non-refundable; they often may be applied to the rental, however.
- Is there a **reconditioning fee**, a stocking fee, or a depreciation fee when you return the instrument?
- Note that stores may ask for a **deposit** or require your credit card details.

Try before you buy

It's also possible to rent a more expensive instrument, so you can take your time to assess its quality. For example, you may rent a forty thousand dollar instrument for six hundred dollars per month, the rental fee equaling 1.5% of the list price.

BUYING A VIOLIN?

If you're looking for a decent, good-sounding violin that you can enjoy playing for a good few years, many dealers and teachers will tell you to spend some eight to twelve hundred dollars or more, and add at least another two or three hundred for a basic bow and a case.

Inexpensive instruments

Of course there are plenty of people who have had years of fun playing a much less expensive instrument. After all, you can buy a complete outfit for as little as three or four hundred dollars, or even less.

That said, there are inexpensive violins that are barely playable unless you have a lot of work done to them — even if they are labeled 'shop adjusted.'

Shop adjustment

Basically, every production violin needs an additional shop adjustment before it can be played. This adjustment, also known as *setting up the instrument*, would include making sure that the bridge, nut, sound post, fingerboard, and tuning pegs perfectly fit the instrument, and other jobs to make the violin perfectly playable.

Better, finer, richer

If you buy a more expensive violin, the higher price typically indicates that more time and attention has been devoted to its manufacture, that higher quality types of wood have been used, and so on.

All this goes to make a better-looking, richer-sounding instrument that may well be easier — and more fun — to play.

Better but less expensive

That said, you may very well find a new six hundred -dollar instrument which performs and looks better than a new one priced at a thousand dollars, depending, for one thing, on where the instrument was made.

A good sound for less

The most important tip when you go to buy your first instrument is to take someone along who knows violins. A proficient violinist or violist will be able to tell you if a violin sounds much better than its price suggests, or the other way around. If you don't know a violinist you can ask to come along, try asking your teacher. And if you can't find anyone at all, at least buy or rent your instrument from someone who can play it for you.

STUDENT AND MASTER VIOLINS?

All kinds of terms are used to classify violins. For example, instruments are referred to as student violins, concert violins, workshop violins, master violins, and so on.

To begin with...

Some classify violins in three groups: student violins, orchestra violins, and concert violins. These terms seem to suggest that you should start off with the first, buy an orchestra violin once you are good enough to play in a large ensemble, and move on to a concert violin as soon as you're ready to play a solo concert. Similarly, there are conservatory and artist violins.

Problem

The problem with these names is that everyone has their own ideas about what they mean. For instance, some master violin makers build 'student violins' that sell for ten times the price of a mass-produced 'concert violin'.

In other words, these terms are often meaningless as well — so don't pay any attention to what an instrument is called. Its price will usually tell you more.

Handmade

'Handmade' is another term that can be misleading. Plenty of low-cost (factory-made) production violins have largely or entirely been built by hand — but that doesn't necessarily mean they're good instruments.

Master violins

The term 'master violin' can be just as vague. Officially, though, master violins are made from start to finish by a master violin maker. They typically cost some ten thousand dollars or more, and the instrument may not be ready in a year or so. It goes without saying that a master violin maker or *luthier* does everything by hand — so you usually won't catch them using the term 'handmade'.

Workshop violins

Workshop violins are typically instruments that others may call intermediate or step-up violins, with prices starting around a thousand dollars. These are often good, handmade instruments, but they're produced in series, rather than by one master luthier.

Old production instruments

Older production violins can fetch relatively high prices, because many violinists believe that old instruments sound better, or simply feel that they're 'the real thing.' Even so, a brand new violin costing eight hundred dollars may well be a better instrument than a twelve-hundred-dollar violin that was built in the early 1900s, for example.

Has to be good

On the other hand, an old and well-maintained factory-made violin that has been played a lot almost *has* to be a good violin. After all, nobody would play a violin much that doesn't sound good or isn't enjoyable to play.

Violas and small violins

Violas are more expensive than violins of the same quality. That's because they are bigger, and fewer of them are made. The same goes for viola bows, strings, and cases. Likewise, fractional-sized violins are not always that much cheaper than full-sized instruments.

True story

A true story. A violinist goes to buy an expensive violin. He plays, looks, and listens, plays and listens some more, and then he makes his choice: This violin is the one for him. He's absolutely sure of it. But he doesn't buy it because, to his shock and surprise, he is told that he picked the cheapest instrument available, priced at only ten thousand dollars — and he was actually looking for a instrument of at least five times that price. It really happened, and not just once...

BUYING TIPS

The main buying tip? Always buy your instrument from people who understand — and love — violins, as they won't send you home with a barely playable instrument. They will also be able to guide you in the sometimes confusing world of the violin, with its numerous (brand) names, names of violin makers, and countries of origin. Chapter 15 tells you more about this.

Where to buy?

You can buy violins in general music stores, which usually sell lower-priced production instruments, or at specialized violin dealers and violin makers. Besides expensive handmade (master) violins, many violin makers sell and rent more affordable instruments as well.

On approval

In some cases you may be able to take an instrument on approval, so that you can assess it at home at your leisure. This is more common with expensive instruments than with budget violins, and you are more likely to be given the option if you are a good violinist than if you are choosing your first instrument.

Label

You can buy a good violin online, through a classified ad or at an auction, if you know what to look for. A word of warning, though: There are thousands of violins that have a labels bearing the name Stradivarius, or the name of another famous violin maker. Anyone can make labels, though. Making violins is a lot harder...

Antonio Stradivarius Cremonenfis
Faciebat Anno 1999

Just about anyone can make a label...

Appraisal

If you find a secondhand instrument anywhere else than at a reputable violin dealer or maker, it's best to have it appraised before you buy.

Violin makers can usually tell you exactly what a violin should cost. They'll also tell you what repairs or adjustments it may need, and what that would cost you. The costs of an appraisal are typically based on the value of the instrument.

Buying online

You can also buy musical instruments online or by mail-order. This makes it impossible to compare instruments. Online and mail-order companies usually offer a return service for most or all of their products: If you're not happy with your purchase, you can send it back within a certain period of time. Of course the instrument should be in new condition when you send it back.

Time

Take your time when you go to buy an instrument. After all, you want it to last you for a long time. Only if you fall in love with a violin or viola should you buy it straight away. Or perhaps a week later, or once you can afford it...

Fairs and conventions

One last tip: If a violin or viola convention is being held in your vicinity, try to attend it. Besides lots of instruments you can try out and compare, you will also come across plenty of product specialists, as well as numerous fellow violinists and violists who are always a good source of information and inspiration.

MORE AND MORE EXPENSIVE

Professional violinists and conservatory students often play instruments worth tens of thousands of dollars, and there are even violins that cost more than a million. How do they get so expensive, and who can afford them?

Like paintings

Violins by famous makers like Stradivarius, Amati or Guarnerius don't cost so much only because they're so good, but also because they are at least three hundred years old: They're rare, just like the famous great paintings from that era.

Better?

Violins seem to improve with age. Still, age doesn't make violins better as much as it does make them more expensive. You can easily pay four times as much — or more — for a high-quality twentieth century instrument as for an equally good new violin.

A modern violin or a Strad?

In blind-fold tests, violinists and other experts have often favored a modern violin over a Stradivarius worth fifty times as much, or more...

Less famous, less expensive

The price of an old violin also depends on how well-known its maker is. For example, you can buy very good, eighteenth century German violins of lesser known luthiers for less than ten thousand dollars.

Reasonable?

When discussing old and expensive violins, terms such as 'good' or 'reasonable' may not mean what you think they mean. For every expert who claims that you can get a 'reasonable violin' for some three to five thousand dollars, there's another who will tell you that 'reasonable' starts at no less than thirty to fifty thousand dollars.

A few years or fifteen minutes

Come to that, some experts say that a new violin will start sounding really good after a few years of playing, while others say it takes fifteen minutes at most...

Conservatory students

Some conservatory students rent their expensive instruments, others can afford to buy one, and still others complete their education with a decent violin that costs just a few thousand dollars. Also, there are foundations that lend expensive instruments to talented students and professional musicians.

5

A Good Violin

When you first start playing, all violins seem to look and sound the same. This chapter shows you the differences between them and tells you how to audition them, covering varnishes and wood, sizes, tops and arches, bridges, necks, pegs – and sound, of course.

How a violin sounds depends a lot on how it was built and on the quality of the wood. But the strings are important too, and so is the bow, and the adjustment of the instrument. These three subjects are dealt with in Chapters 6, 7, and 11 respectively.

Purely by ear

The first and major part of this chapter is about everything there is to see on violins and violas, and what it all means for how they sound. If you prefer to choose an instrument using your ears only, then skip ahead to the tips on pages 57–61.

The looks

Violins come in glossy and matte finishes, and some instruments have a warm, satin-like glaze. When it comes to their color, there are even more variations. Some are pale orange or even yellowish, others have a rich amber or a deep brown hue, and still others tend toward red or purple. Some companies also make violins in bright, solid colors.

Oil and spirit

Traditionally, violins have an oil-based finish, which used to take weeks to dry. Today, these finishes can be dried using ultraviolet light, and you may be able to find oil-varnished violins for as little as three or four hundred dollars. Spirit-based varnishes are used on violins in most price ranges. Be aware that spirit- and oil-based finishes on inexpensive instruments tend to be quite brittle.

Invisible repairs

No one finish is typically better than any other. What's really important is that both oil-based and spirit-based varnishes basically allow for invisible touch-ups. So does nitrocellulose lacquer, when applied properly.

Synthetic varnishes

Low-priced violins can have a synthetic finish (i.e., polyurethane) too. This glossy type of finish can be applied very quickly, using spray guns. It's also strong, hard, and easy to clean. Being so hard, on the other hand, it may reduce the instrument's sound potential, especially when applied very thickly. Another drawback of this type of finish is that it doesn't allow for invisible repairs.

Shading

Violins are not always the same color all over. Older violins sometimes have lighter patches where they have been handled a great deal.

These worn-out patches are sometimes imitated on new violins too. This technique, known as *shading*, makes a violin look older than it really is.

Checked finish

Older violins often have a *checked finish*, the varnish being marked with a fine web of tiny cracks. This effect, also known as *craquelure*, can be imitated by the maker too. Yet another way to make an instrument look older is to bring out the grain by applying a dark dye.

Aged to order

Antiquing is a generic name for making a violin look older — and often more expensive — than it is. If you have an instrument custom-built, you can of course ask the violin maker to 'antique' it for you. Even minor damage, small repairs, and worn-out spots can be imitated.

Flamed wood

The wood of the backs and ribs of many violins looks like it's been licked by flames. This *flamed*, *figured* or *curled wood* is common on more expensive violins, but you may find it on budget instruments also.

Flames, sound, and price

Whether the wood is plain, or slightly, medium, or well flamed does not relate to its quality or sound potential. On the other hand, beautifully flamed wood has its price. In student and intermediate price ranges the highly flamed instruments are often the most expensive ones.

A bookmatched, flamed back

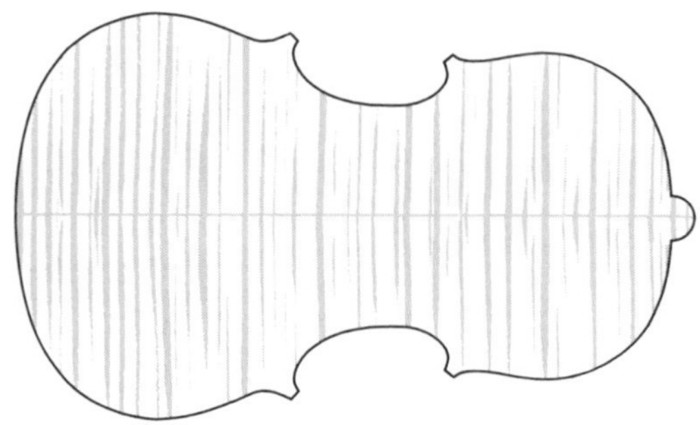

Bookmatched

Many flamed backs clearly show that they're made up of two very precisely mirrored or *bookmatched* halves (see page 160).

Fine or clumsy

Most scrolls look like a perfect spiral, with sharply carved, smooth edges. Others look more clumsily carved. Are these violins no good? No: Clumsy volutes may even be rarer on mass-produced instruments than on hand-carved violins.

A perfect spiral, or a clumsy job...

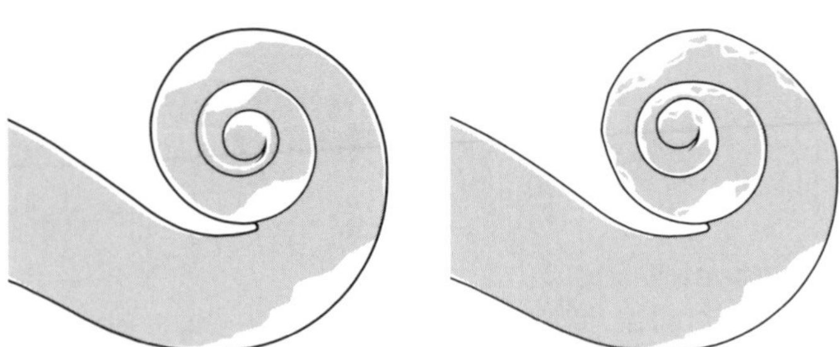

Slightly different

Every volute is slightly different, from maker to maker and from brand to brand. The more you look, the more differences you will see. One example would be the *fluting*, i.e., the carved grooves in the back of the volute.

Purfling

The inlaid purfling, usually consisting of three strips of wood, is not just for decoration. It also protects the instrument, preventing cracks at the edge from extending to the *plates* (top and back). Double purfling is rare, but you may come across it. A tip: On budget violins, the 'purfling' may be painted onto the wood.

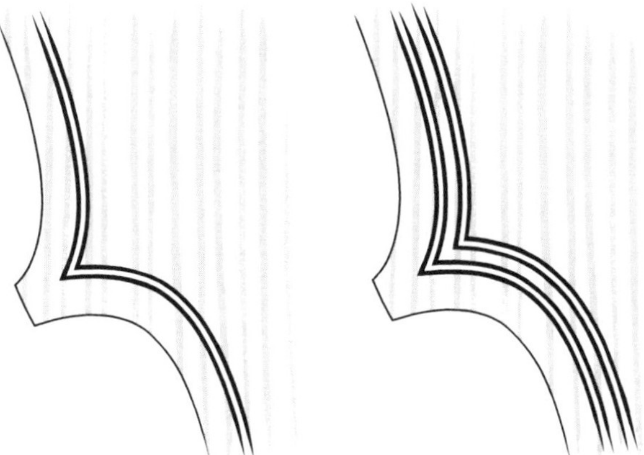

Purfling usually consists of three or more inlaid strips of wood.

THE BODY

The body of one violin may be a little higher or wider than another, or a little slimmer at the waist, or the top may be slightly more or less arched. What does this do the sound?

(Not) all the same

Full-size violins are all pretty much the same size, to the nearest fraction of an inch. Full-size violas, however, come in sizes from 15" to 17" (body length) in half-inch increments. Most adult violists use a 16" or 16.5" viola.

Larger

There are beautiful small violas around, but usually a larger model will sound both 'larger' and fuller — which is what most violists prefer. If you like or need a smaller one, you may want to look for an instrument that's a little wider and deeper. This would make it more likely to sound like a 'real' viola.

Stop

When trying out violas, you may find yourself sounding *flat* (too low) in certain positions. This happens mainly on larger instruments, typically due to the fact that the instrument has a deviant *stop*, *f-stop*, or *mensur ratio*. These technical terms refer to the relationship between the distances from the nut to the top edge of the body, and from the top edge to the notches in the *f*-holes (see *String length*, page 210).

Slimmer waist

Learning to see the subtle differences between one violin and the next takes time, patience, and practice. Some instruments have noticeably wider bodies than others, or just a wider or a slimmer waist (the *C-bout*). This hardly affects the sound, but it can make one instrument easier to play than the other.

Stradivarius

Many of today's violins are still based on the instrument that Stradivarius designed around the year 1700. Other models are often named after the luthiers who introduced them. Again, the differences are small, but they're well documented. A Stradivarius model is a little wider and has shorter *f*-holes than a Guarnerius model, for example.

The top

The top is the most important part of a violin. When you play, the strings make the top vibrate, and it is mainly these vibrations that determine the sound of your violin. This is why the top is often referred to as the soundboard of the instrument.

Spruce

The top, also known as *table* or *belly*, is almost always made of a solid piece of spruce, which has been carved into shape. Spruce is also used for the bass bar and the sound post.

Maple

The back is usually made of one or two pieces of solid maple, a slightly heavier and denser type of wood. Student violins may have a laminated back, made up of several plies. Maple is used for the ribs and the neck as well.

Fine grain

Violinists often prefer the top to have a grain that is straight, even, and not too wide, getting gradually finer toward the center of the instrument. Of course, some violins have a beautiful grain but don't sound good, and there are great sounding violins with an uneven, wide grain as well.

The arching

A top with a lower arching will often help produce a stronger, more powerful sound than one with a high arching. Most violin tops are between 0.6" and 0.7" (15–18 mm) high. The back is usually a little flatter.

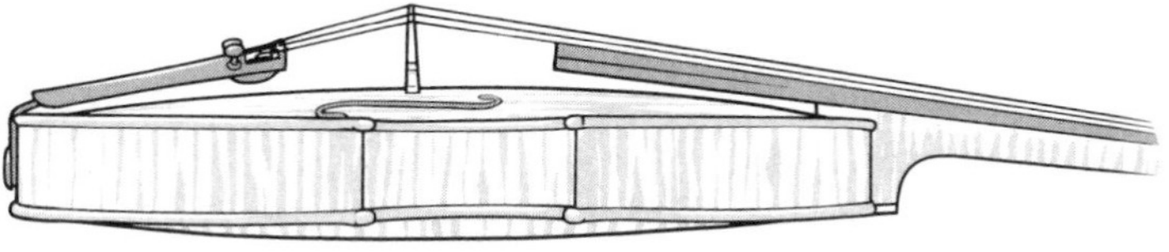

The back is a little flatter than the top.

The channel

A violin with a deep, broad channel will often have a softer sound than an instrument that barely has this 'valley' along the edge.

Flowing lines

You can spend hours looking at violin archings. They all look similar, yet they are all slightly different. It is important that the arch has a flowing shape, that there are no flat parts or odd angles, and that the arching isn't too high, too low, or too narrow. The more often you look, the more you'll see.

Thick and thin

Low-cost violins and violas often have thick tops, which are easier to make. A top that is too thick will make for a thin sounding instrument. Master violin makers measure the thickness of a top to hundredths of an inch, making the instrument produce the sound they have in mind.

Graduated top and back

Good instruments have a *graduated* top and back, the exact thickness of the plates varying from spot to spot.

The ribs

In a full-sized violin, the ribs are usually a little over an inch high all the way around. A relatively shallow instrument is likely to sound thin, and a violin that is too deep may have a hollow sound. Violas are often deeper by the tailpiece than they are at the neck end.

Hot hide glue

Violin makers use hot hide (animal) glue for their instruments. Joints — or *seams* — fixed with this type of glue can be loosened again if necessary. This allows a violin maker or technician to remove the top for repairs.
Low-cost production violins may use types of glue that prevent such repairs.

NECK AND FINGERBOARD

The neck and fingerboard affect both the playability and sound of a violin. They can also tell you something about how well-made the instrument is.

Ebony

Fingerboards are almost always made of ebony. This is a nearly black, extremely hard type of wood. The smoother and more even the fingerboard, the more easily it will play.

Softer wood

Low-cost violins sometimes have fingerboards of softer, light-colored wood, which may be painted black to make it look like ebony. Such fingerboards can sometimes be recognized by lighter patches or blank spots on the sides.

A new fingerboard

After years of use, even the hardest fingerboard will wear, after which it should be reworked or, eventually, replaced (see Chapter 11, *Violin Maintenance*).

Thick fingers

The grooves or notches in the nut, at the top of the fingerboard, determine the string spacing and the string height at that end. Nuts can be replaced to adjust both string spacing and height. For example, if you have thick fingers, you may prefer a nut with grooves set a little further apart.

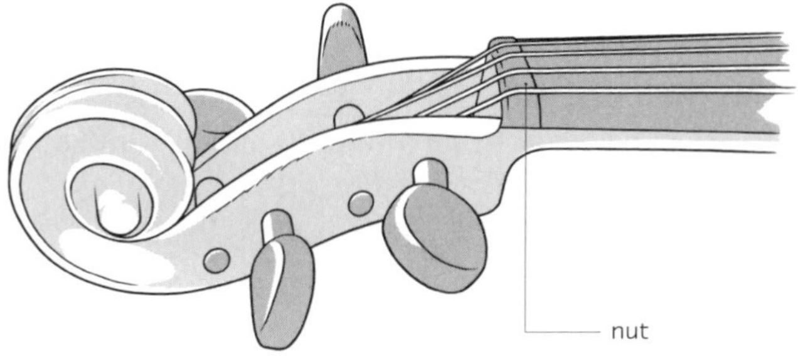

The nut can be replaced.

Feel the neck

Necks are always much lighter in color; a dark neck would soon show worn patches. On more expensive violins, the wood is usually not varnished but protected with a little oil. See if the curve of the neck fits your hand nicely and check the neck for odd pits or bumps. Note that necks come in different thicknesses.

Concave fingerboard

The fingerboard is very slightly concave along its length. This prevents the strings from buzzing when playing in the higher positions.

The fingerboard: slightly curved.

Straight

If you look at the neck and fingerboard lengthwise, they should of course be straight, and set exactly in the center line of the violin. The neck should not look as though someone has tried to wrench the instrument out of shape.

In between the notches

If you hold the violin with its tailpiece toward you, you can check whether the bridge is exactly between the two notches of the *f*-holes. If so, then check that the strings run perfectly straight along the fingerboard.

Downwards

If you look from the side, you'll see that the neck is tilted slightly downwards. This used to be different: Pre-nineteenth century instruments have a 90-degree angle between the neck and the side of the body. This made these instruments produce less volume,

A smaller neck angle gives a bigger sound.

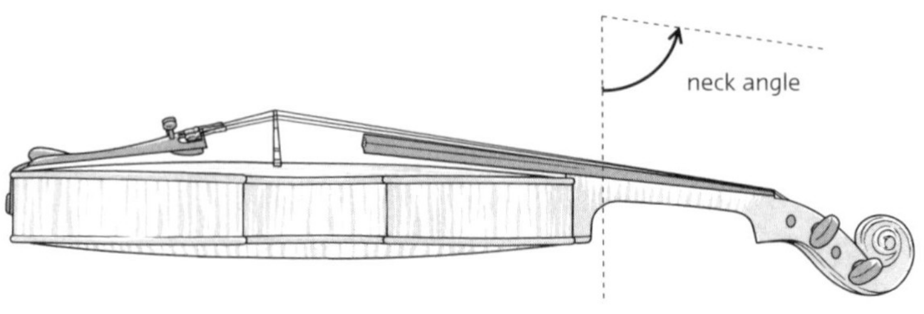

as the larger neck angle reduces the pressure of the strings on the bridge. Conversely, a smaller neck angle increases string pressure on the bridge, making for a bigger, louder, or more radiant sound.

Baroque violins

To play music from the Baroque era (ca. 1600-1800), violinists often prefer to use a special Baroque violin. The softer, mellow sound of these violins is due to a larger neck angle and other factors, including the use of gut strings (unwound, except for the G) and a different string length. Baroque violins are played without a chin rest.

STRING HEIGHT

The *string height* or *action* refers to the distance between the strings and the fingerboard. Having your strings too high above the fingerboard makes playing uncomfortable.

If string height is too low, the strings may buzz against the fingerboard. In between, it's largely a matter of taste and the type of strings you're using. A greater string height (also referred to as a *higher action*) can give your instrument a slightly clearer, brighter, more powerful sound.

Room to move

The distance between your strings and the fingerboard increases from the nut to the other end of the fingerboard, where string height is measured. As you will see, the thick strings always have a slightly higher action: They need more room to move than the thinner ones.

The figures

On a violin, the E-string usually is some 0.12" (3 mm) above the fingerboard, while the G-string will be at about 0.16" to 0.20" (4–5 mm). Gut strings need a higher action, while steel strings are

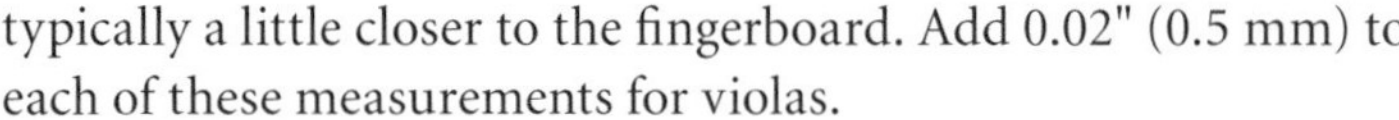

typically a little closer to the fingerboard. Add 0.02" (0.5 mm) to each of these measurements for violas.

Too high

If you have a new violin that has not yet been properly adjusted, the strings will probably be too high. This can be fixed by having the bridge and/or the nut lowered or replaced.

THE BRIDGE

The bridge affects both string height and the sound of the instrument.

Straight

Bridges are a bit slanted at the front and straight at the back. The straight back must be perpendicular to the violin's top, and the bridge's feet should be exactly between the notches of the *f*-holes.

Flecked

Some bridges are plain, while others show highly flecked or speckled wood, called *Spiegelholz* in German. This characteristic of the wood doesn't reveal its quality. Non-flecked, slightly flecked, and highly flecked wood is used for both cheap and expensive bridges. Ideally, the wood should have a fine, straight grain.

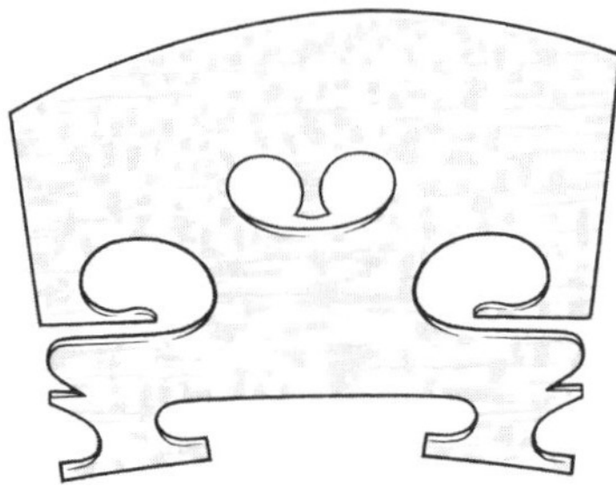

A flecked bridge: cheap or expensive...

(Un)treated

Violin catalogs often indicate whether bridges are treated or untreated, which refers to the bridges being finished with varnish or oil. Some feel that this treatment enhances the quality of the bridge; other experts prefer to use untreated ones.

Bridges and sound

A relatively heavy bridge will muffle the sound of the instrument slightly, just like a mute does (see pages 98–101). A very light bridge may be the culprit if a violin has a very thin, weak, or uncentered tone. The hardness of the wood also plays a role. A bridge made of harder wood helps produce more volume and a stronger, brighter tone.

Models

Bridges come in different models, but you'll need to look very carefully to tell them apart. Violin makers and technicians do see those differences, and they know which bridge is best for your instrument.

Blanks

The bridges you find in stores and catalogs are blanks: Bridges always need to be custom-fit to your instrument. There are bridges with moveable feet that automatically adjust to the arch of the top — but even if you prefer this type of bridge, it can't hurt to have a specialist install it: Properly fitting a bridge to an instrument involves more than carving the feet (see also page 141).

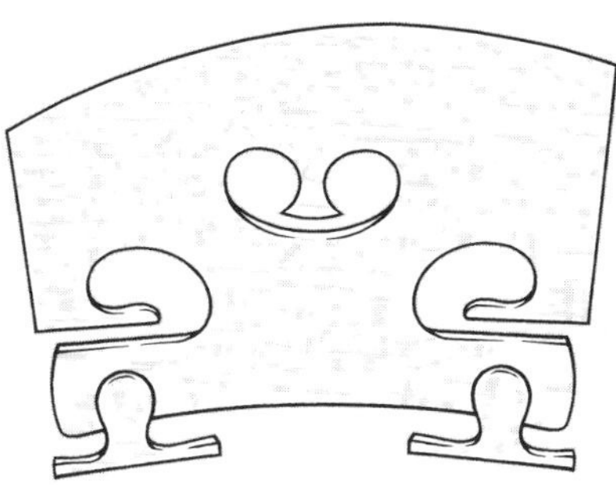

An adjustable bridge with moveable feet.

Not too deep

The longer you play your violin, the further the strings will wear into the bridge. If the grooves become too deep, the sound will be muffled and it will be harder to tune the instrument. String height will be decreased as well, and strings may break sooner. Ideally, the grooves should be just so deep that two-thirds of the thickness of each string sticks out above the bridge.

Cutting string

The E-string, at no more than 0.01" (0.25 mm) thick, is the one most likely to cut into your bridge. That's why some bridges have a piece of bone or hardwood set into them at this point. Two alternatives are a plastic sleeve around the string (see page 73) or a piece of vellum underneath it (parchment; see page 138).

A bridge with an ebony inset.

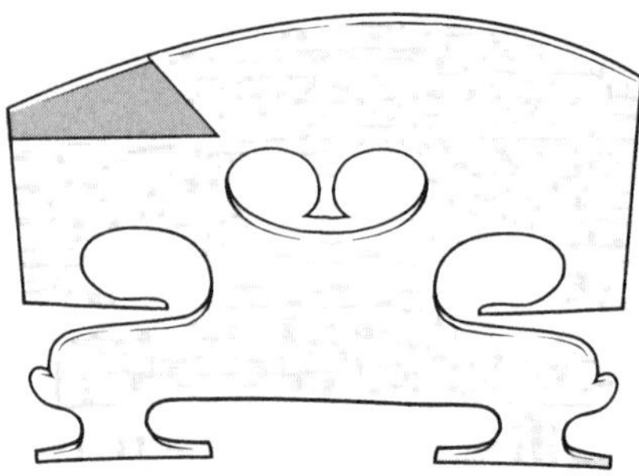

Two at once

The top of the bridge has almost the same curve as the top of the fingerboard, so it is highest in the middle and lowest by the thinnest string. Beginners often prefer a highly-curved bridge: The higher curve reduces the chance of inadvertently bowing two strings instead of one. Conversely, if you want to be able to play two or even three strings simultaneously, you will need a bridge with a lower curve.

Sagging bridges

In time, string pressure will make nearly all bridges sag. A violin will produce its best sound with a straight bridge — so have your bridge replaced in time (see page 140).

Height and tone

The bridge height influences both string height and tone. A slightly higher bridge increases the string tension, which makes the sound a little brighter or stronger. If the bridge is too high, the sound may become a little hollow. In some cases a high bridge is used to compensate for a very modest neck angle.

Bridge height

Most bridges are between 0.12" and 0.14" (31–35 mm) high at their topmost point.

THE SOUND POST

Inside the body, slightly behind the bridge, is the sound post. This spruce rod and its placement are essential for the sound of your violin or viola. French violin makers even call it *l'âme*: the soul of the instrument.

Fractions

The sound post must be straight, and long enough to be firmly wedged between the top and the back, but not so long that it pushes these plates apart. Its exact position is critical too, measured to less than a twentieth of an inch (1 mm).

Adjustment

A violin maker can adjust the sound of a violin by altering the position of the sound post. This way a violin can be made to sound slightly less edgy, or a little brighter, for example. Also, if one string sounds louder or softer than the others, having the sound post repositioned may be the solution, balancing out the volume of the individual strings. Alternatively, you may try using different strings — but that's another chapter (Chapter 6, to be precise).

PEGS AND FINE TUNERS

You can tune a violin with the wooden tuning pegs at the top. Depending on the strings you use, for one thing, you'll use the fine tuners in the tailpiece as well, or instead. Both pegs and fine tuners come in different types and sizes.

Hardwood

Pegs get thicker toward the thumb piece. This tapered shape helps the pegs to hold. They are usually made of ebony, the type of wood that is also used for tailpieces and chin rests. Rosewood and boxwood are popular types of wood as well. Rosewood has a reddish-brown color; boxwood is usually yellowish. *Tip:* A violin with a 'full-ebony trim' has ebony parts all over.

Breaking strings

Very cheap violins sometimes have pegs made out of a softer type of wood, into which the strings will wear grooves. When a string jams in such a groove, it is very likely to break some time soon.

A good fit

Cheap violins are often hard to tune, or they go out of tune

Tuning pegs.

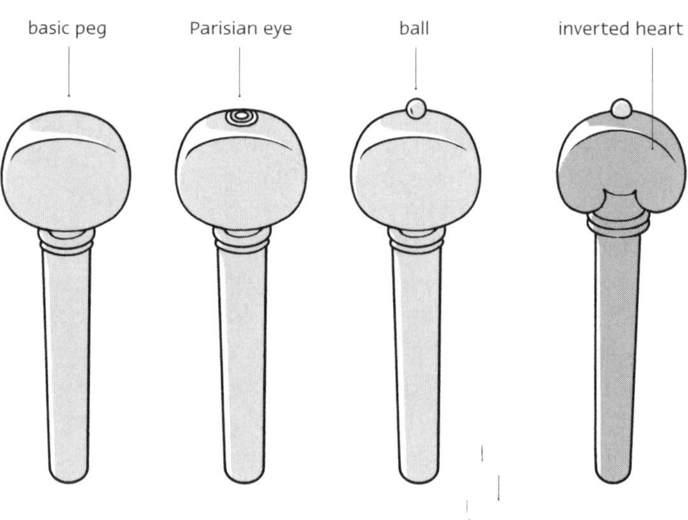

quickly because the pegs are of poor quality or don't fit properly. Tuning pegs should turn easily, but not slip.

Parisian eyes

Pegs come with various peg head designs, such as inverted heart shape with a ball on top. Another type of decoration is the *Parisian eye*: a small, mother-of-pearl dot with a metal ring around it. A single mother-of-pearl dot is simply called an *eye*, *single eye*, or *eyelet*.

Fine tuners

Certain types of strings (e.g., steel strings) can best be tuned with *fine tuners*. That explains why less expensive instruments, which usually come with steel strings, typically have four of these miniature tuning machines built into the tailpiece. Fine tuners are available separately too. Many violinists combine three gut strings with a single steel string (high E), for example, and they'll use a fine tuner for that steel string only.

Tipcode VIOLIN-006

This short video demonstrates the use of a fine tuner.

Fine tuners and synthetic strings

Fine tuners can be used for some types of synthetic strings as well, but not for all of them: The strings may be too thick to fit the fine tuner, or the fine tuner may cause string breakage.

Names and lengths

Fine tuners come with many different names (*adjusters*, *tuning adjusters*, *string tuners*, *string adjusters*...) and in different shapes and sizes. Longer models stick out a little from below the tailpiece. If you use short ones, you won't see much of them besides the thumb screws. Some well-known models of short fine tuners include the Hill model, the Uni, and the Piccolo.

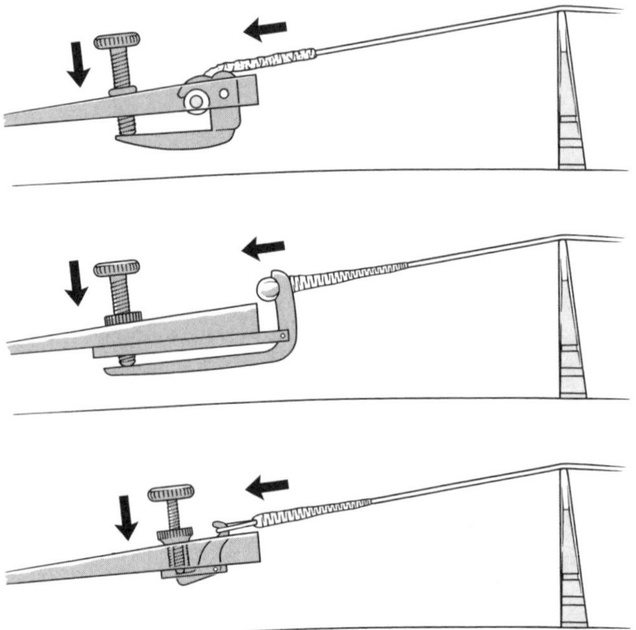

A built-in fine tuner (above), long and short fine tuners.

Easier

Long fine tuners make tuning even a little easier than shorter models. Fitting new strings becomes easier too. If the tailpiece of the violin is very close to the top, perhaps because the top has a high arch, you can be better off with short ones: Long fine tuners may damage the top when turned too far. Some models have a pad to help prevent such damage.

Short or long

There are violinists who prefer short fine tuners because long ones reduce the length of the string between bridge and tailpiece, which they consider bad for the sound. There are at least as many good violinists who can't tell the difference.

Loop or ball

Most strings have a ball at the end that fits the fine tuner. Steel E-strings come with either a ball or a loop. Ball-end strings require a fine tuner with two prongs, while loop-end strings can be attached to both one and two-prong fine tuners.
There are also special fine tuners for gut strings, and models with an extra wide slot for heavy-gauge strings: Using a thick string in a narrow slot may result in string breakage. Fine tuners are very affordable items. They typically cost some two to five dollars each.

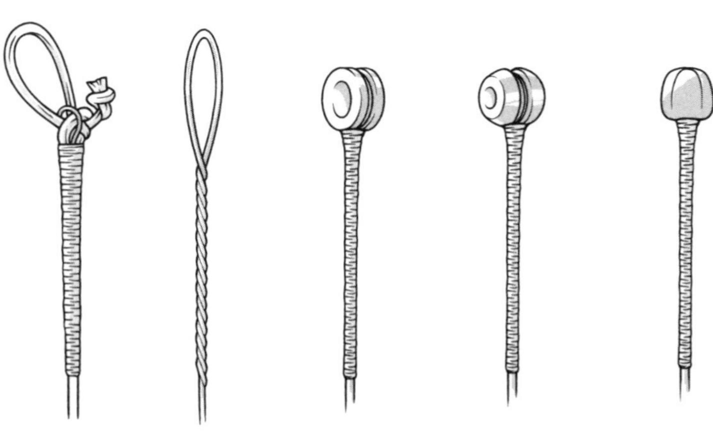

Some strings have a loop, others a ball end.

Geared pegs

Rather than using fine tuners, you may have a modern type of tuning mechanism installed, which incorporates a built-in gear system. These geared pegs or planetary pegs provide a 4:1 reduction: four turns of the peg head make the shaft of the peg go round just once. This allows for much finer tuning than a conventional wood peg.
Geared pegs can't stick or slip, and they are virtually maintenance-free. The sound of the instrument may improve as well: after all, tailpieces were not designed with fine tuners in mind. Getting rid of the fine tuners also reduces the risk of buzzing and rattles.

TAILPIECE

The tailpiece, believe it or not, also influences the sound of your instrument. Tailpieces come in various materials and designs, and with or without decoration or built-in fine tuners.

Slim or angular

There is a great variety of tailpieces available, especially in wood. Two examples of well-known basic designs would be the French model, with a very slim upper section, and the Hill model, named after a British manufacturer, with elegant lines and an angular end.

A French model tailpiece...

... and a Hill tailpiece.

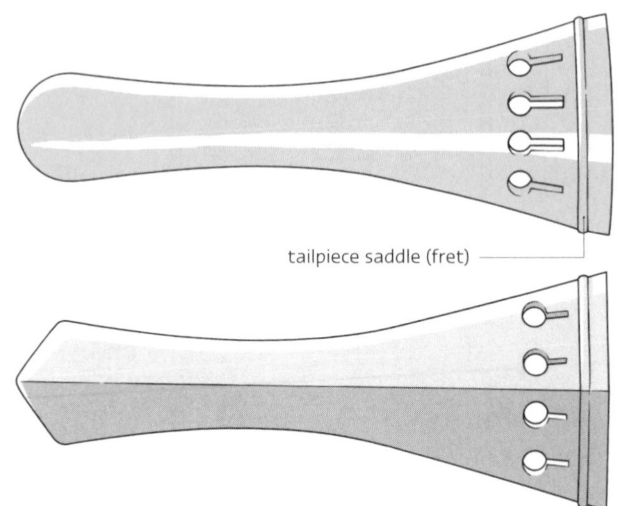

Parallel

The strings should always run parallel between the bridge and the tailpiece. If not, the tailpiece is too narrow or too wide for the instrument.

Golden saddle

If you have gold-plated or brass fine tuners, you might like the *tailpiece saddle* or *fret* to have the same appearance. Usually, this little ridge is black. Other decorations on tailpieces include a Parisian eye or an inlaid figure.

The sound

The tailpiece has roughly the same effect on the sound of the violin as the bridge. That means that a heavy tailpiece will slightly muffle the sound, making it a little less bright, somewhat similar to what a heavy bridge (or a light mute) would do. Conversely, a lighter tailpiece promotes a clearer, brighter timbre. If it's too light for your instrument, it may however yield an uncentered, thin tone. Do note that a light-weight bridge may have that same effect.

All together

Of course, these differences are not that obvious — but having a heavy tailpiece with four large fine tuners too close to the bridge can make your instrument sound noticeably duller, the extra mass acting as a mute.

Viola tailpieces

Because violas come in different lengths, viola tailpieces do too. It's important to have one that is the right length for your instrument, as this length determines the important string length from the bridge to the tailpiece (see page 141). Check the bottom of the viola tailpiece for the size viola it's made for.

AUDITIONING THE INSTRUMENT

If you try ten violins in a row, you'll have forgotten what the first one sounded like by the time you try the last. The following tips make it easier to compare violins.

Take it with you

If you already have a violin, take it with you when you go to choose another instrument. Comparing it with a different violin makes it easier to judge what you hear.

If you have your own bow, take that with you too. Otherwise, use the best bow available in the store, or the best one you're allowed to use. Using a good bow will give you a better idea of what the different violins are capable of.

Someone else

If you don't play yourself, or have only just started, you won't know whether an instrument has a poor sound, or whether it's just you. So ask someone who does play to demonstrate the different violins to you. That someone could also be the violin maker or the salesperson, for instance.

By ear

If you ask someone else to play, you can also hear how the violin sounds from a distance. The sound will be quite different compared to having it right by your ear. Another tip: If you simply can't choose between a few violins or violas, turn around. Then you won't know which instrument is being played, so you'll really be choosing only by ear. You won't see the price tag, the finish, the brand name, or the age anymore. Sometimes musicians choose much cheaper instruments than they expected to by ear — but it may be the other way around too.

Get to know the extremes

Start by listening to two very different violins, one with a bright sound, and one with a mellow, dark sound. Knowing these extremes will make it easier to find the instrument you truly like.

Three

First, make a rough selection of the instruments you like on first hearing. Take three of them, and compare them with one another. Replace the one you like least by another violin from your first selection. Compare the three again — and so on.

Play something simple

If you have a lot of violins to choose from, it's often easier if you only play briefly on each one. Play something simple, so that you can concentrate on sound and the playability of the instrument, rather than on what you play. Even a scale will do. When you have a few violins left, and you really need to choose, you'll probably want to play longer and more demanding pieces of music so that you can get to know the instruments better.

Sheet music

If you're not used to playing by heart, bring a small selection of sheet music with you. Select some pieces that you really master, so you can focus on how the violin makes the music sound, rather than on the notes.

String by string

You can also compare violins string by string or note by note. How does the open E-string sound? Do all four strings sound equally loud, and how does the instrument sound in the highest positions? How do they sound when you pluck them, or when you play long notes?

Same pitch

The violins that you are comparing should be tuned properly and — of course — to exactly the same pitch. If not, one violin might sound a little warmer than the others, say, just because it is tuned a bit lower. For similar reasons, you should really only compare instruments that are fitted with the same type of strings. If not, you will be comparing strings rather than violins.

LISTENING TIPS

It's impossible to put into words how different violins sound, if only because such words mean different things to different people. Still, the following tips will make choosing an instrument by ear a lot easier.

Volume and projection

Some violins will always sound very soft or weak, however energetically you play them. In an orchestra with one such instrument, no one will be able to hear you. Other violins can be heard at a fair distance too, even if you play very softly. A violin like that has good projection.

Even

The E-string not only sounds higher than the other strings, it also sounds different. If you play an E first on the open E-string, and then play the same pitch on the A- and D-strings, you'll hear that very same pitch sound with three very different *timbres.* All the same, a violin should have an even, balanced sound: The differences from string to string should not be like going from one instrument to another.

Response

A violin should have a good response. That means it sounds good and responds immediately, even when you play very softly. If not, the instrument is hard to play; it makes you really work for each note. If a violin has a poor response, it takes a little while before the tone is really 'there.' On violas, the C-string is very critical, as it's so heavy.

Uncentered tone

On some violins, the sound never seems to gel. They lack foundation, producing an uncentered, weak tone. Both a slow response and an uncentered tone can also be due to the strings, to the bow, to the rosin, or — sadly — to yourself.

Dynamics and colors

A violin should be able to sound just as loud or soft as you play. If it does, it has good dynamics. If it doesn't, its performance will always be a bit shallow. The instrument should also be able to produce different timbres or 'colors'. One example: If you play a little closer to the fingerboard, the sound is supposed to become noticeably rounder than if you play near the bridge — and the instrument should sound good both ways.

Preference

Apart from that, sound is mostly a matter of personal preference. Bear in mind that when two people listen to the same instrument, they'll probably use different words to describe what they hear. What one finds harsh or edgy (in other words, unpleasant), another may describe as bright and clear (in other words, pleasant), and what's warm to one ear sounds dull to another. It all depends on what you do and do not like — and how you put that into words.

Rich = more of everything

The better an instrument is, the richer it sounds. Richer means a full, resonant tone; it means there's more of everything; and it means that you're allowed to produce a wide variety of tonal colors, mellow and vivid, subdued and bright, sad and happy, shaded or direct…

Poor

Some words associated with poorer-sounding instruments are nasal (as if the violin has a cold), hollow (like you're playing in a bathroom), thin (as if it's a miniature), or dull (as if there's a blanket over it) — and everybody has more or less the same idea of what those words mean.

USED VIOLINS

When you go to buy a used instrument, there are a few extra things you should remember.

Repairs

First of all: No matter what's broken, a decent violin can almost always be fixed. Of course, if you decide to buy an instrument that needs some work, you need to know what it's going to cost first. Some types of damage are easy to see, others require an expert eye to be discovered. Come to that, you need to be an expert to judge things like how well a violin has been repaired. If in doubt, have the instrument appraised first (see also page 34).

Major damage: cracks in the sound post and bass bar areas.

Checklist

Here are some of the main things to check when buying a used instrument. A complete list would soon be too long for this book.

- Violin **varnish wears**. One place to check is where your left hand touches the body. If the varnish has completely gone, you may need to do something about it.
- If the type of varnish allows for it, it is usually **touched up** after repairs (see page 38). Make sure this has been done properly.
- Check the **edges**. This is where the instruments gets knocked most often. Depending on the damage, repairing damaged edges can cost up to hundreds of dollars.
- Cracks in the top or the back always run lengthwise. Cracks in **the sound post and bass bar areas** are often hard to see and even harder to repair.

Cracks in the cheeks and the shoulder of the neck.

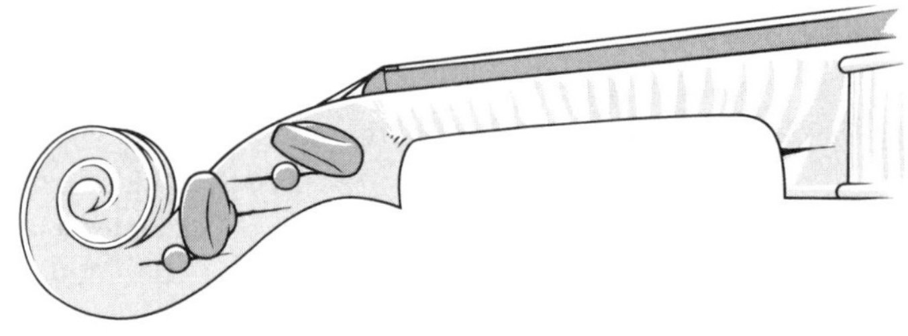

- Other places to check for cracks include the **shoulder** of the neck and the **cheeks** (sides) of the pegbox near the pegs.
- Glue can come loose — along the edges for instance, or at the neck. Tap a violin very softly with a knuckle. This can sometimes help you discover **loose glue joints**.
- If the **tuning pegs** are pushed very far into the pegbox, sticking way out at the other end, they may need to be replaced, and the holes may need to be rebushed. This is quite expensive.
- Check the **arching of the top**. Sometimes the pressure of the strings makes the top a little flatter near the bass bar, or a little higher by the sound post.

Woodworms

Woodworms burrow into wood and leave narrow tunnels. This can be very serious, especially if they have been at work in the top or the back. You won't find woodworms in a instrument that has always been played: This particular animal doesn't like music (i.e., vibrations). If you want to know whether they're still around, lay your instrument on a piece of black cardboard overnight. If there's sawdust on the cardboard the next day, the instrument has tenants.

6

Good Strings

For hundreds of years, all violin and viola strings were made of gut. These days you can buy steel strings and synthetic-core strings as well, in many variations. Every type of string produces a different sound, some strings are easier to play than others, and some strings sound better on one violin or viola than on another.

Violin strings can last a long time — up to a year, or even longer. It does help if they are fitted properly and kept clean. More information on keeping your strings in good condition is in Chapter 11, *Violin Maintenance.*

Gut, steel, synthetic

There are three main types of strings. Originally, violins had gut strings exclusively. Then came steel strings, which sound a lot brighter. Strings with a synthetic core didn't appear until the 1950s, but they are now the most widely used type.

Important

Strings are very important for how your violin or viola sounds and plays. The difference in sound between cheap and expensive strings can easily be much bigger than the difference between a cheaper and a (much!) more expensive instrument. The same is true for the difference between synthetic-core, steel, and gut strings.

Expensive

Try different strings once in a while, and consider trying really expensive strings too, if only once, even on an affordable instrument. You may be surprised by the effect they have on the sound.

Winding

Most violin and viola strings are wound with ultra-thin metal ribbon. Because of this winding the string itself can be kept fairly

A wound string.

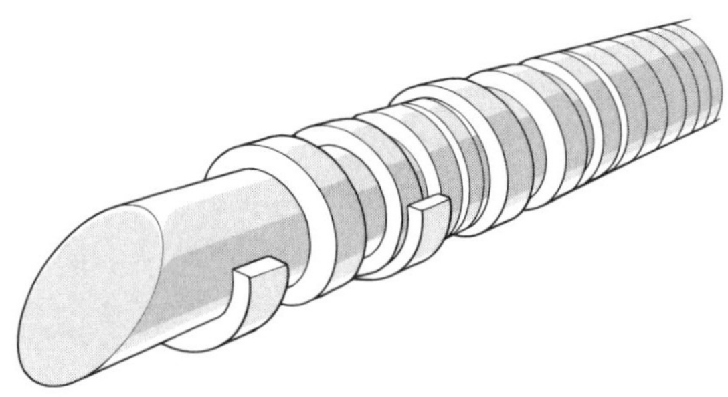

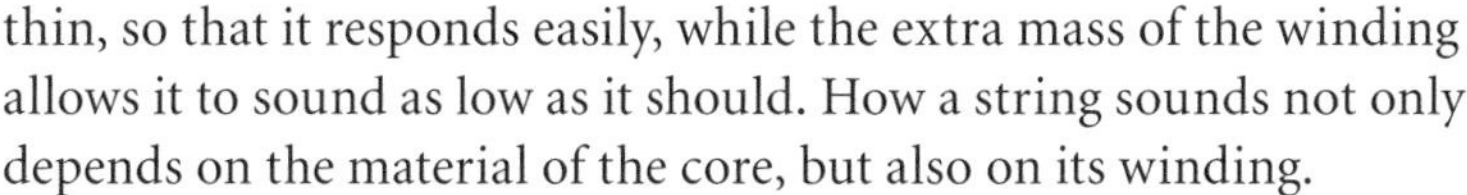

thin, so that it responds easily, while the extra mass of the winding allows it to sound as low as it should. How a string sounds not only depends on the material of the core, but also on its winding.

Hard and soft

Finally, there is also a difference between 'hard' and 'soft' strings, or strings with a higher or lower tension, and between thicker and thinner strings.

This chapter tells you what you need to know about these important differences.

Prices

The prices mentioned below are for sets of four violin strings. If you buy strings separately, the thickest string will often cost two, three, or four times as much as the thinnest. Viola strings usually cost five to fifteen dollars more per set of four.

GUT STRINGS

The first violins had sheep gut strings, and there are still violinists who feel that the instrument sounds best with this type of strings. Of course gut strings are also used when playing music from the time that these were the only strings available (see page 47, Baroque violins).

Sound

The sound of gut strings is often described as mellow, warm, complex, and rich. They allow for great variation in color and inflection — which in turn demands a good musician. Gut strings need to be broken in. It takes a few hours of playing to get them to develop their full sound.

Tuning

As they stretch a fair bit when new, you'll have to tune gut strings quite often at first. Additional tuning is also required as gut strings detune with changes in temperature or humidity.

Expensive

Gut strings, which are used mainly by professional musicians, often don't last very long and are generally quite expensive. A set will easily cost forty to fifty dollars or more, but they're available for less as well.

Steel E

Gut E-strings are quite rare as they are very vulnerable. Even so, they are still used by some musicians, for instance those who play Baroque music (seventeenth and early eighteenth century). Most other violinists prefer to use a steel E.

Wound E or plain E

There are wound, steel E-strings, but they're usually *plain strings.* A plain steel E-string typically sounds a little clearer than a wound one.

STEEL STRINGS

Steel strings offer a clear, bright, powerful sound and an immediate response. They're very reliable and they last a long time, typically from six months to a year, or even longer.

Bright

Their ease of response makes steel strings a good choice for beginners, but there's more. Because of their bright tone, steel strings sound especially good on violins which themselves have a slightly subdued sound. They're also popular with violinists who need a lot of volume and a strong, big sound.

The core

Most steel strings have a core made up of several very thin steel strands. Strings with a solid steel core help produce a stronger

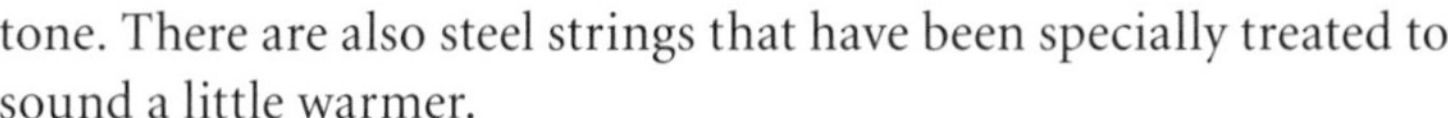

tone. There are also steel strings that have been specially treated to sound a little warmer.

Advantages

Steel strings have two more advantages. First, they do not have to be broken in: They sound good immediately, and they're not as stretchy as new gut or synthetic strings. Second, steel strings are not bothered by changes in temperature and humidity.

Plenty of volume

Sets of steel strings are available for around fifteen dollars or even less, which is why most cheaper violins come with this type of strings. Professional-quality steel strings may cost up to three times as much.

The E

There are more variations on the steel E-string than on any other, with prices from one to ten or more dollars. They can be either wound or plain. (The other steel strings are always wound.) Steel E-strings can also differ in thickness and in stiffness, or the precise material used may be different.

Chrome-steel or coated steel

For example, ordinary steel easily discolors and may go out of tune as it does. You can get around this problem by using a chrome-steel string. Or you can buy an E-string with a coating of silver, gold, or another material.
This ultra-thin finish protects the steel and also promotes a slightly warmer sound.

SYNTHETIC STRINGS

Synthetic-core strings are the most widely used, by beginners, students, and professional string players. You could consider them 'in between' gut and steel, in terms of tone, life expectancy, and price. A set of four typically costs twenty-five to thirty-five dollars, but they come cheaper or twice as expensive as well. The most expensive synthetic strings cost more than affordable gut strings.

Sound

There's a large variety in synthetic-core materials and windings, so there's a large variety in the sound of synthetic strings as well. Generally speaking, their timbre is close to that of gut strings, but it's a bit brighter or livelier. Compared to steel strings they sound noticeably warmer — or less hard and bright… The core material is typically perlon or another type of nylon.

Breaking them in

New synthetic-core strings may sound a bit harsh at first. If so, their sound will improve after a couple of hours of playing. They're a bit stretchy too, so they need time to settle in. Another similarity with gut strings is that synthetic strings are often combined with a steel E-string.

WINDINGS

To make sure that the strings of a set fit together as well as possible, manufacturers often use different windings within one set of strings — silver for the G, for instance, to add a little power to this thick string, and aluminum for the next two strings, to make them sound a bit warmer.

Viola

You'll come across all kinds of combinations for violas too. Two silver and two aluminum-wound strings, perhaps, going from thick to thin. Or one silver, one chrome, and two aluminum-wound strings.

Wound steel

With steel sets, the strings will often have the same winding. Nickel or aluminum wound strings will usually make for a softer, sweeter, or warmer sound than chrome-steel windings.

Windings and string life

The type of winding also affects the life expectancy of your strings.

Two examples? A titanium winding makes for longer lasting strings, titanium being both very hard and corrosion-resistant. Aluminum-wound strings tend to wear out faster, as the winding is relatively soft.

More

There are many more materials used to wind strings, including copper, titanium, tungsten, and silver mixed with gold. If you are looking for a particular sound, a good salesperson or violin maker will be able to help you with your choice. But if you really want to be sure, you'll need to try out different strings for yourself. The same goes for choosing between thicker and thinner strings, or between louder and softer-sounding strings.

LOUD OR SOFT

Synthetic and steel strings often come in several varieties, often indicated with the Italian terms *dolce* (soft), *medium*, and *forte* (strong). You may also see German descriptions like *weich* (soft) and *stark* (strong). Forte strings, also indicated as *orchestra* or *solo*, are heavier than dolce strings.

Lower tension

Softer-sounding strings have a lower tension than louder strings. Some string manufacturers describe their strings by their tension, marketing low-, medium-, and high-tension strings. Strings with a higher tension take a little more effort to play and they respond less quickly, but their brighter, stronger sound enhances the projection of your instrument. Medium strings are the most commonly used.

The instrument

Which strings are best also depends on the instrument you are playing. Using forte strings may work great on one violin, but their higher tension may actually degrade the sound on another instrument, for example.

Colors

To indicate the different types of strings, manufacturers use colored thread at one of the string's ends. At the other end, the string's pitch has been marked with another color, to prevent you from putting the D-string where the A-string should be, for example.

Confusing

Unfortunately, no uniform color codes are used, so the same color may mean one thing for one make and something else for the next. Similarly, there's no consistency in what (string type, string pitch) is indicated at which end of the string. Confusing...

The same make and series

If the strings on a violin are of the same make and series, you will see four different colors (the pitch of each string) at one end, and only one color (indicating the type of strings) at the other.

Mixed up

If this is not so, there's a fair chance that strings of different brands, series, or tensions have been combined in one set. If they all sound good and sound good together, that's no problem. If you want to know which strings are fitted to your instrument, ask an expert. They can usually tell from the color codes.

Thick or thin

Gut strings come in different gauges. Heavier-gauge strings are harder work to play; they may sound fuller, louder, and clearer; and they don't respond as easily as thinner strings.

How thick

If you want to know exactly how thick a gut string is in inches, divide its gauge by 500. For example, a 14 is 14÷500 = 0.028". To get millimeters, divide the gauge by 20.

TIP

String height

Fitting higher-tension strings will increase the instrument's action. Conversely, lower-tension strings will decrease the action, as the strings reduce the tension on the neck. Adjusting string height — by means of replacing or lowering the bridge, for example — is a job for a professional.

AND MORE

A few final tips about ball ends and loops, about how long your strings will last, and about plastic sleeves and string brands.

Ball or loop

As discussed on page 55, steel E-strings come with either a loop or a ball at the end where they attach to the fine tuner. Check your fine tuner to see which type you need.

Write it down

If you're putting new strings on your violin, you can list their details on page 219 of this book. This allows you to buy the same strings if you like them, or avoid them if you don't.

How long

How long your strings will last depends on many things — on how often you play, of course, but also on the core material of the strings and the type of winding, on how well you keep your strings clean, and even on your type of perspiration. Various types of windings don't take well to acidic perspiration, for example.

Sleeves

Strings often come with small plastic sleeves. These prevent the strings from cutting into the bridge, and they prevent the bridge from damaging the strings. Most of the sleeve must be on the side of the tailpiece; otherwise it will muffle the sound too much.

E-string

That said, a little muffling may actually be desirable with a steel E-string, making it sound just a little sweeter. Being so thin, the same string is also the most likely one to cut into the bridge.

Tone filters

Rubber *tone filters* are available separately. Some companies include them with their strings. A small piece of rubber (gasoline) tubing under the string does the same job.

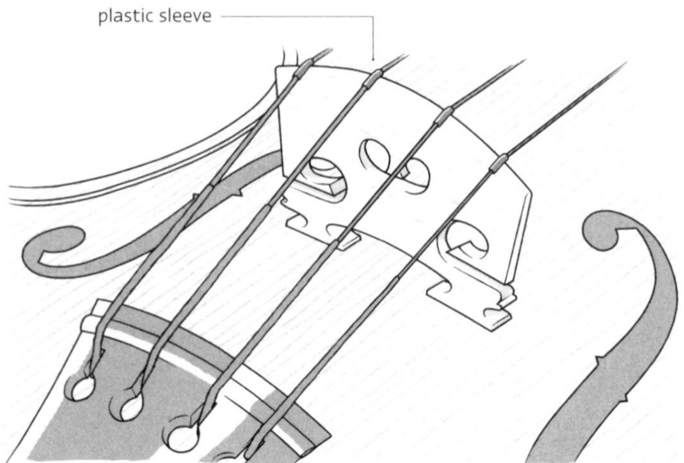

Plastic sleeves around the strings.

Fractional sizes

Fractional-sized instruments require fractional-sized strings. Regular strings will not provide the required tension, resulting in a weak tone and possible string breakage.

Which strings?

If you're looking for a certain timbre or trying to balance the sound of your instrument by fitting other strings, for example, don't hesitate to consult your violin maker or dealer. Also visit string makers' websites; some of these sites provide excellent information on the characteristics of the various types of strings they make.

String brands

Choosing the right strings can also be hard because of the wide selection that is available. The three best known string makers are probably D'Addario (USA), Pirastro (Germany), and Thomastik-Infeld (Austria), each of which makes various series of strings. If you look just at some of their synthetic and steel strings, well-known examples are the Pro Arte and Helicore series from D'Addario, Tonica, and Chromcor (Pirastro), and the Thomastik Dominant and Spirocore series. Among the many other bowed string companies are Corelli, Jargar, John Pearse, Kaplan, Larsen, Mathias Thoma, Meisel, Pinnacle, Prim, Pyramid, Stellar, Supreme, Syntha-Core, and Super-Sensitive. Some of these companies also produce rosin, other accessories, or even instruments.

Custom strings

Some violinists and violists prefer to put together their own sets of strings, combining a variety of brands, series, materials, and windings to produce a specific sound or effect, and to optimally adjust the instrument to their demands.

An octave lower

Ready for something completely different? By fitting a set of *octave strings* or *baritone strings*, you can make your violin sound an octave lower. These strings, produced by various string makers, are mostly used in experimental, avant-garde music. Your violin will need to be adapted to accept these special strings, which are considerably thicker than regular strings.

7

Bows and Rosins

Your bow should suit your instrument, your style of playing, and the music you play. A chapter about brazilwood and pernambuco, synthetic bows, frogs, ferrules, horsehair or synthetic hair, weight and balance, and rosin.

The stick of the bow can be made of wood or a synthetic material, with wood still being the most popular choice. Most cheaper wooden bows use brazilwood; more expensive bows are made of pernambuco.

Brazil or pernambuco

So, for around two hundred dollars you can buy an 'expensive' brazilwood bow or a cheap pernambuco bow. If two bows cost the same, choose the one that suits you and your instrument best — whichever type of wood it's made of.

Synthetic bow

Instead of wood, the stick may be made of a synthetic material — carbon fiber or fiberglass, for example. The cheapest models, available for fifty dollars or even less, are designed mainly for children. These bows are very durable and don't need much care or attention. Professional synthetic bows are also available, and they can cost thousands of dollars.

Synthetic hair

Low-priced bows often come with synthetic hair. This provides less grip than the traditional horsehair, and it'll never make the instrument sound its best.

Bleaching

Some manufacturers bleach the bow hair to make it look bright and white all over. However, bleaching is said to reduce the durability of the hair.

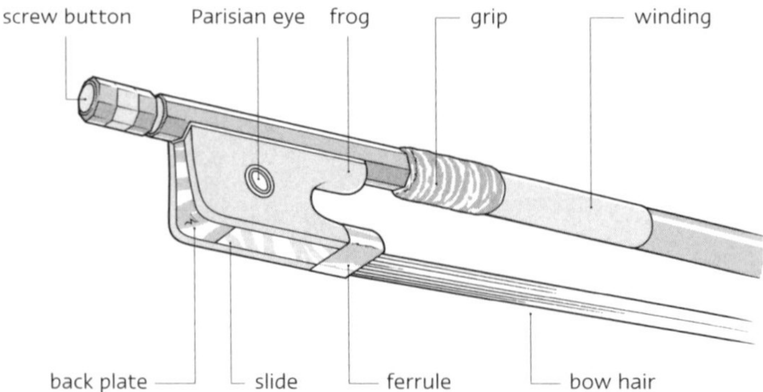

The mountings

A bow's *mountings* are its metal parts, such as the screw button, the *back plate* of the frog, and the *ferrule* or *D-ring*, where the bow hair enters the frog. The material used for the mounting often indicates the price and quality of the bow.

> **Silver, gold, and nickel silver**
>
> *Silver-mounted bows start at around three hundred and fifty or four hundred dollars, and gold-mounted bows easily cost five times as much. Cheaper pernambuco bows are usually nickel silver-mounted.*

No silver

Contrary to what you might expect, nickel silver does not contain silver. The alloy is also known as *German silver* or *alpaca.*

Full-lined

The frog in the picture on the previous page is a *full-lined frog.*

Half-lined frog

A *half-lined* frog does not have the back plate behind the slide or extending underneath the slide.

Fractional-sized bows

Of course, you can also buy smaller bows for smaller violins and violas (see pages 16–18), in similar fractional sizes, ranging from an almost full-sized ⅞ to bows as small as 1/32. Fractional bows usually have brazilwood or synthetic sticks.

Viola bows

Because violas are larger, you'd expect viola bows to be longer — but they're not. In fact, viola bows are often about 0.2" (5 mm) shorter than violin bows. Even so, they are a bit heavier (see page 84): A lighter bow wouldn't get the strings of a viola to vibrate enough.

CLOSE UP

Of course, there is more to a bow than the type of wood used and the mountings — the shape of the stick, for one thing, and the decorations on and around the frog.

Eight-sided or round

The bow stick, also known as the *shaft*, gets gradually thinner from the frog to the head. It can be either round or octagonal (eight-sided). Some violinists feel that an octagonal stick makes a bow play better, as they may be a little stiffer or more stable than round sticks.

A little more

A bow with an octagonal stick usually costs a little more than one with a round stick — not because it's necessarily better, but simply because it takes more work to make one.

Frog

The frog, named after a part of a horse's hoof with the same shape, is usually made of ebony. Cheap sticks sometimes have plastic frogs. The slide, at the bottom of the frog, usually has a mother-of-pearl finish. The frog itself is often decorated with single or Parisian eyes; intricately carved and decorated models are also available.

Screw button

The screw button is often inlaid. Expensive sticks may have costlier decorations, sometimes with single or Parisian eyes on each side of the octagonal screw button. Screw buttons also come

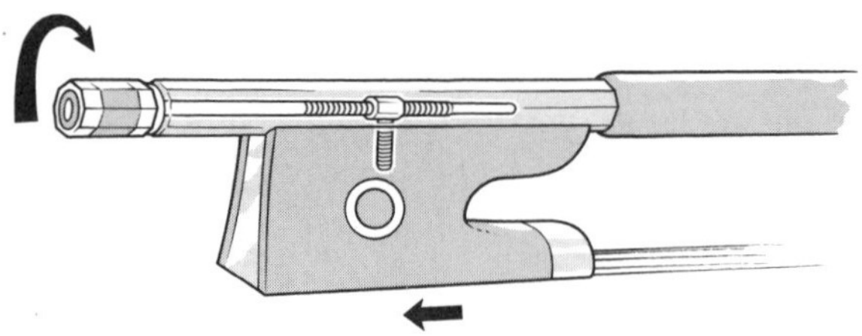

This is how you move the frog by turning the screw button.

in two- and three-part versions (i.e., silver-ebony, and silver-ebony-silver respectively).

Brand name

Usually the make of the bow or the name of the maker or the brand is literally branded into the wood of the stick, just above the frog.

Bow grip

The leather bow grip, *thumb grip* or *thumb cushion* may be a little thinner on one stick than the next, and some models have tiny 'ventilation holes.' Instead of leather, vinyl or plastic is sometimes used on less expensive bows. This may feel a little sticky when you're playing, and it may even slide out of place.
If you feel that the bow grip is too thin, you can have a thicker one installed, and vice versa. Eventually, bow grips wear out and need to be replaced.

Winding

Silver thread is usually used for the winding or *lapping*. Some bows have a silk winding or synthetic imitation baleen windings in one or two colors. The use of real baleen (whalebone) has been banned.

Head

In the past, the protective *face* at the other end of the stick was usually made of ivory. Today, bow makers typically use a synthetic material, metal, or bone.

THE BEST BOW

How much should a bow cost, and which one is the best? There are no straightforward answers to either of these questions.

The price

Some violinists say your bow should cost as much as your violin. Others say half as much, or a quarter — so that's not much help. Your best bow is the one you feel most comfortable with and that helps you to make your instrument sound its best, for a price you can afford.

Suitable

Which bow suits you best depends on your bowing technique and on the music you are playing. A bow must suit your instrument too, and the strings you are using — so always try out bows with the instrument you are playing.

More expensive

As with violins, a more expensive bow is not always better, and an antique or vintage bow will often cost a lot more than an equally good new one. You can also get lucky and find a great bow for a bargain price. Even top violinists may have a 'cheap' bow in their collection because it's perfect for certain pieces of music.

Suit the music

Again, the bow should suit the style of music you play. Violinists often use a different bow for older music, say from the Baroque era, than for more recent works. Typically, they will own a variety of bows. Some bows are better for a bright, clear tone; other bows are preferable when the music requires a mellow timbre.

CHOOSING A BOW

When you've tried out ten bows in a row, you'll have forgotten what the first one sounded and played like — just like violins. It's often easier if you concentrate on, say, three bows, after a first rough selection. Reject the one you like least, then take another one to compare the other two with. And so on. First play short, simple pieces, or even just scales, and play longer pieces when you have just a few bows left to choose from.

What to play

Of course, the best test for any bow is to play the music you intend to use it for. Try out all the bowing styles you know. Play slowly, fast, loudly, and softly, while focusing on performance of the bow and the sound it helps you create. Some bows respond better to the way you play and to where exactly you bow the strings than other models — again, just like violins.

Sound

A different bow will make you sound different, just like another instrument. Brighter or warmer, heavier or lighter, fuller or thinner, softer or louder... In fact, there are even small differences between every two 'identical' bows — especially if they're wood models. These nuances will often come out best if you play slow phrases, and you'll hear more of them when playing bows and instruments in the higher price ranges (and when you're a better player!).

Curve

A bow should be curved so that the hair, when slack, just touches the middle of the stick. If the stick is more curved than that, the hair may touch it when playing. Such 'strong' bows can also feel a little restless or jumpy.

Camber

A bow that is too straight — a bow with too little *camber* or curvature — on the other hand, may be sluggish. Looking on the bright side, you could also say that a bow with a lot of camber would be good for *spiccato* (in which the bow bounces lightly off

Tipcode VIOLIN-007

This Tipcode clearly demonstrates what spiccato looks and sounds like.

the strings), while a fairly straight bow would be better for slower phrases and legato playing. But then, a really good bow should allow you to play anything...

Flexibility

If you take a bow by both ends and bend it carefully, you can feel how flexible or elastic it is. A very flexible bow can make it difficult to play fast pieces, but it may have a better tone than a stiffer model. Playing may be easier with a less flexible bow, but producing a good, long tone may become trickier. After all, flexibility is important for string contact. *Tip:* There are synthetic bows that allow you to adjust their flexibility so you can match it to your technique or the music you play.

Weight

A full-sized violin bow usually weighs between 2 and 2.3 ounces (57–65 grams). Viola bows are a bit heavier, as said before. They typically range from 2.3 to 2.65 ounces (65–75 grams).

Heavy or light?

If you're looking for a full-bodied sound, you may want to find a relatively heavy bow. Lighter bows are often better suited for a lighter sound. If a bow is too light, it won't make the strings vibrate enough and you won't produce much sound at all.

Small

Even the smallest weight differences can influence how you sound and play. Some musicians can spot a difference of a gram or two.

Balance

The heavier a bow is at the head end, the heavier it will feel. To check its balance, make sure the hair is slack. Hold the bow

Top-heavy

A top-heavy bow may be easier to guide. A bow with the weight further back feels lighter, but you have to guide it more.

between your thumb and forefinger, at about ten inches (24.5 cm) from the end of the stick itself, not including the screw button. If the head goes down, you're holding a top-heavy bow.

Response

With some bows, the tone builds up very gently and gradually, and with others the strings respond very quickly. To check the response of a bow, play lots of short notes on the lowest strings. Most violinists like to have a bow with an even response — in other words, a bow that produces the same response from the strings in the middle, near the head, and near the frog.

In line

Look along the back of the bow, from the frog, to check that it is straight. Just like a violin neck, the bow must not look as though someone has tried to wring it out.

Hair tension

When comparing bows, take the hair tension into account. The 'best' tension may vary per bow, depending on the elasticity of the stick and your personal preference, among other things.

Starting point

As a starting point, you may want to check the distance between the middle of the stick and the hair. If this is about 0.4" (1 cm), the tension will usually be about right — unless the stick has a deviant curvature, for one thing.

Different per bow

Turning the screw button the same number of times for each stick isn't a good starting point, as this will probably result in very different hair tensions per bow.

Temperature and humidity

A tip: The number of times you need to turn the adjustment screw may vary on your own bow depending on the humidity and temperature. For example, low humidity will make the stick slightly stiffer, so the bow hair will be at the right tension sooner, and vice versa.

Secondhand bows

A few tips if you're planning to buy a used bow:

- If the hair is **overstretched**, a bow will feel very sluggish. The solution is to have the bow rehaired (see page 132).
- Another problem with overstretched bow hair is that the frog needs to be shifted very far back. This **changes the balance** of the stick.
- A bow can lose some of its **curvature** or camber over the years. It may be possible to restore it, but be sure you know whether your bow is worth the expense.
- What Stradivarius is to the violin, François **Tourte** (France, 1747-1835) is to the bow. If you find his name on a bow, it probably won't be a real Tourte, unless it has a price tag of fifty thousand dollars or more.

Brands

A few well-known bow brands are Dörfler, Höfner, Paesold, Seifert, Student Arpège, Roger, Werner, and W.R. Schuster. Low-cost synthetic bows are made by Schaller, Glasser, and other companies; Berg, Coda, and Spiccato make more expensive and professional synthetic bows too.

Small

Bows are also produced by numerous smaller workshops, for example in Brazil, with prices from around four hundred dollars. Bows by independent makers, who work alone, typically start at around a thousand dollars. If a bow doesn't have a brand name at all, it's likely a very cheap one.

ROSIN

Bow rosin makes the bow hair slightly sticky so it can properly 'grab' the strings and make them vibrate. When you play a string, the rosin makes it stick to the bow hair — until the tension gets too high as you move the bow along. At that point, the bow hair lets the string slip for a split second. This *stick-slip motion* is what makes the string vibrate.

Many stories

String players often use the same type of rosin for years, but experimenting a bit can't hurt. A tip in advance: There are many stories about the differences and similarities of rosins, usually contradicting one another. Trying rosins out yourself is the best thing you can do.

Hard

Each rosin cake comes wrapped in a cloth or in a box so you're less likely to touch the rosin itself. Rosin is not only sticky, but also quite hard. As a rule, a cake will easily last you a year or longer, unless you drop it: Being as hard as it is, it may shatter into a zillion pieces.

Light and dark

Many companies sell rosins in two colors, at the same price: a light, honey-like color, and a darker color, almost like licorice. You may read that light rosins are harder and less sticky (so you should use these in the summer, when the higher temperature will make them softer). This may be true of some brands, but it can be the other way around just as well. Often, only the color is different. When you start playing, that difference vanishes as well: Rosin dust is always white.

Rosin is sold in cloths and boxes, rectangular or round blocks, and in various colors.

Harder and softer

The rosin of one brand may be harder than that of another, and some brands sell rosin in different hardnesses. You may be able to feel the difference between the softer and harder types by pressing your fingernail into them.

The best rosin?

Even experts don't agree on which rosin to choose. A few examples of their differing opinions? Softer rosin makes your strings respond better, but because it is stickier, it's more likely to produce unwanted noise. You are less likely to get that type of noise if you use steel strings. On the other hand, rosin developed for steel strings is often harder than rosin designed for gut strings, supposedly because gut strings don't respond properly if you use a very hard rosin…

Loud music, hard rosin?

Some experts — musicians as well as rosin makers — say that harder rosins are especially suitable for louder music, or when a fast response is required, or when the music you play requires a lot of bow pressure. However, other experts recommend harder types of rosin for quiet pieces; being less sticky, they would produce less noise.

Sticky

An extra-sticky rosin tends to produce less dust, so less gets onto your instrument. What's more, you won't need to apply as much pressure on your bow. On the other hand, this type of rosin is more likely to clog up your bow hair, which will then have to be cleaned more often. Some more expensive rosins, having finer particles, are said to produce more — and finer — dust.

Electric strings

There are special bow rosins for electric violins, which are said to contain traces of metal that increase the conductivity of the strings.

Barely noticeable

Many experts believe the biggest difference between the many types of rosin is the amount of dust they produce during application and just afterwards: Once you are playing, the

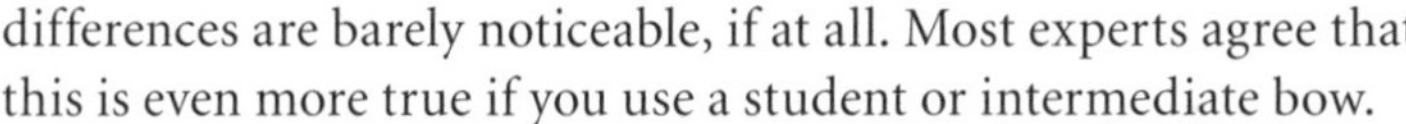

differences are barely noticeable, if at all. Most experts agree that this is even more true if you use a student or intermediate bow.

Confusing

Just to add to the confusion, the very same rosin is sometimes sold with a different package, label, price, and description. And while some manufacturers sell different rosins for violin, viola, and cello, others make just one for all three instruments — and some even produce special types of rosin for electric string instruments.

Gold and silver

Rosins often cost between five and fifteen dollars, including varieties that contain gold or silver particles. The precious metal is said to add clarity and brightness to the sound — but not all players can tell this subtle difference. Some companies offer various types of rosin aimed at beginning players, frequent players, and professionals respectively.

New bow or strings

If you buy a new bow you may well need a different rosin to do it justice, and the same is true if you start using a different type of strings. Some manufacturers try to make it easier for you to match their various types of strings and rosins by producing rosins that bear the names of their strings. This can be useful, though it doesn't mean that it isn't worth experimenting with other brands and types too.

Hours

Unfortunately, trying out rosins is a slow process: The old rosin

Non-allergic rosin

If you're allergic to traditional rosin, try one of the hypo-allergenic or non-allergenic rosins available, or try a rosin that produces less dust. A hypo-allergenic rosin is less likely to cause a reaction, and non-allergenic rosins should not cause an allergic reaction at all.

will still be effective for several hours of playing after you've applied a new one. That's why violinists who use different rosins for different styles of music also have a different bow for each type of rosin — or a different type of rosin for each bow...

Fittings, Mutes, and Cases

As a violinist or violist, your two most important accessories are a properly fitting chin rest and a comfortable shoulder rest. Some of the other main accessories for your instrument are mutes and cases.

Apart from a chin rest and a shoulder rest, the violin's fittings or trim also include the pegs and a tailpiece, which were dealt with in Chapter 5.

Chin rests

The German composer and violinist Louis Spohr introduced the chin rest in the early 1830s. Older violins may show a lighter shade in the chin rest area, where the chins of former owners have worn away most of the varnish.

A different chin rest for every chin.

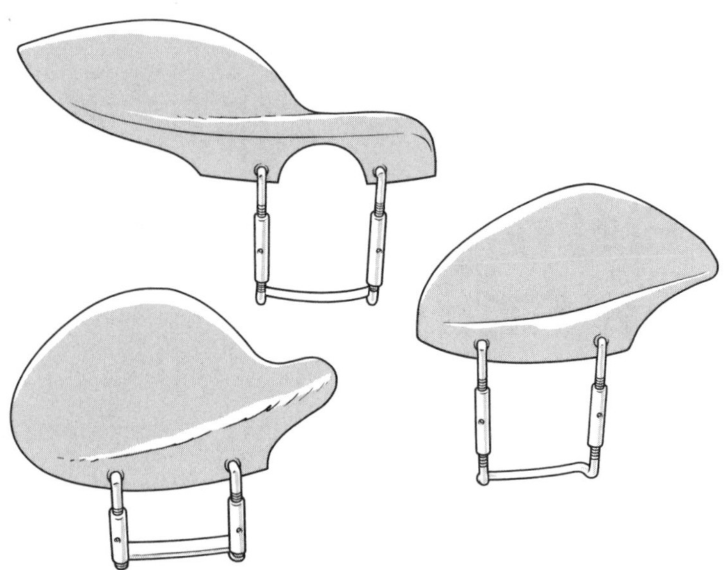

The shape of your chin

The shape and size of your chin determines whether the cup of your chin rest should be large and deep, or small and shallow, for example. Chin rests vary in height too.

Beside or above

Also, you can choose a chin rest that sits right above the tailpiece, or next to it, or somewhere in between. Some types of chin rest allow you to make that choice. The closer the chin rest is to the tailpiece, the more your violin will be in line with your body when you play, and vice versa.

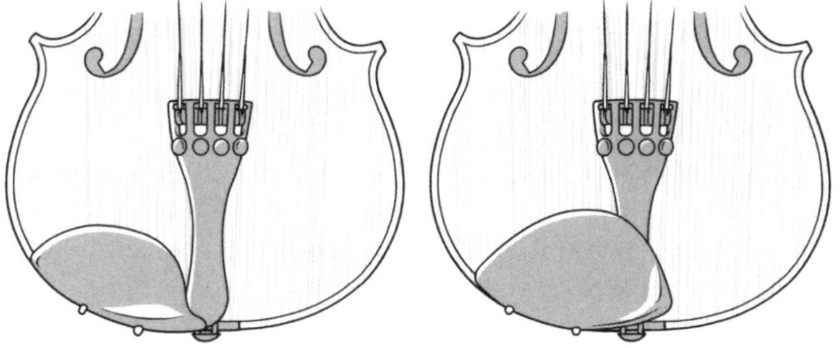

Chin rests in different positions.

Names

Chin rests usually bear the name of their designers, but they're named after cities too, or after famous violin makers (some of whom were long dead when Spohr introduced this useful accessory...).

Plastic, ebony, jacaranda

Many models are available in different materials. You may find a plastic version of a certain model for less then ten dollars, while the same model in wood can cost five times as much. Expensive chin rests, selling for fifty dollars or more, are usually made of costlier woods, such as ebony, rosewood, boxwood, or jacaranda.

Wood or synthetic

If you perspire rather heavily, a chin rest with a wooden cup will probably be more comfortable than a synthetic one. If the wood appears to irritate your skin, you'll probably be better off with a chin rest with a synthetic cup. If you don't know whether it is the wood, the varnish, or something else that's causing the problem, try using a cotton cloth over the chin rest for a while — some violinists always play that way. You can also buy chin rests with a

Nickel

If you develop a rash, it may also be that you're allergic to the (nickel or nickel-plated) metal fittings of the chin rest. Non-allergenic chin rests are available.

soft, leather pad. Some people think they're great, others find that they get too hot for comfort.

Match your violin

Many violinists prefer a chin rest that matches the type and looks of their tailpiece, as well as the finish of body. If you do too, it's worth knowing that you can buy ready-made sets with a chin rest, a tailpiece, tuning pegs, and even an end button in the same color and style.

The chin rest may be attached to the left of the end button, or using one clamp on either side.

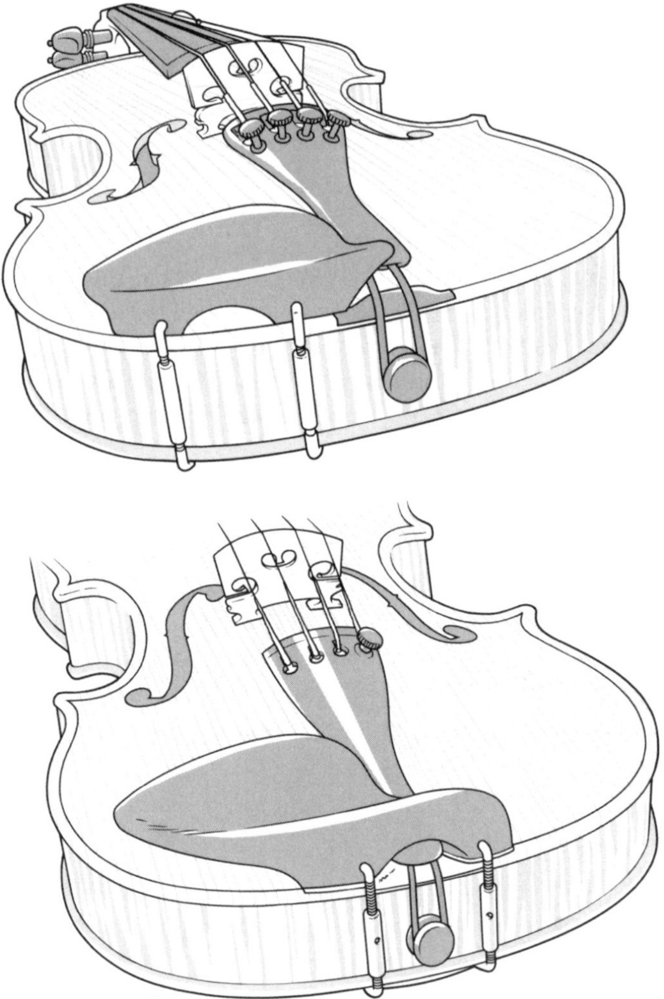

Two clamps

Most chin rests attach to the instrument with two clamps. You can tighten or loosen them with a paper clip, but a special chin rest wrench or key helps to prevent damaging the body. Some chin rests can be set with screws.

Where

Both clamps can be attached to the left of the end button, or there's a clamp on either side. The latter type may be preferred as this places the clamps close to the bottom block (this is the small wooden block that holds the end button; see page 161), making for a secure fit.

Too tight, too loose

A chin rest only touches the violin at the edges. To prevent damage, its clamps are covered with cork. If a chin rest is put on too tight, you risk deforming the ribs, or even the plates. If it's too loose, it could slip off.

Small and large

Of course, there are special chin rests for fractional-sized violins and for violas. In both cases, there is slightly less choice.

SHOULDER REST

The shoulder rest is an even more recent invention than the chin rest. It has only been widely used since the 1950s, and it's still frowned upon by some.

Higher

Using a shoulder rest means that your instrument will sit a little higher on your shoulder, so you don't have to tilt your head as far. On the other hand, you do need to lift your right arm higher, which sometimes causes pain or other symptoms. A lower type of shoulder rest together with a higher chin rest can help avoid such problems.

Pads and wooden rests

Some violinists still prefer the simplest shoulder rest of all: a small cushion or pad, or even a special sponge, the latter selling for no more than a couple of dollars. Others use the traditional wooden shoulder rest, covered with cloth and held in place with rubber bands.

Wide variety

Shoulder pads come in a wide variety of shapes and materials, attached with rubber bands, leather straps, or a combination of both. If you have a long neck, go for a slightly larger model. Also available are inflatable cushions, so you can decide yourself how thick and hard it should be.

Inflatable shoulder rest.

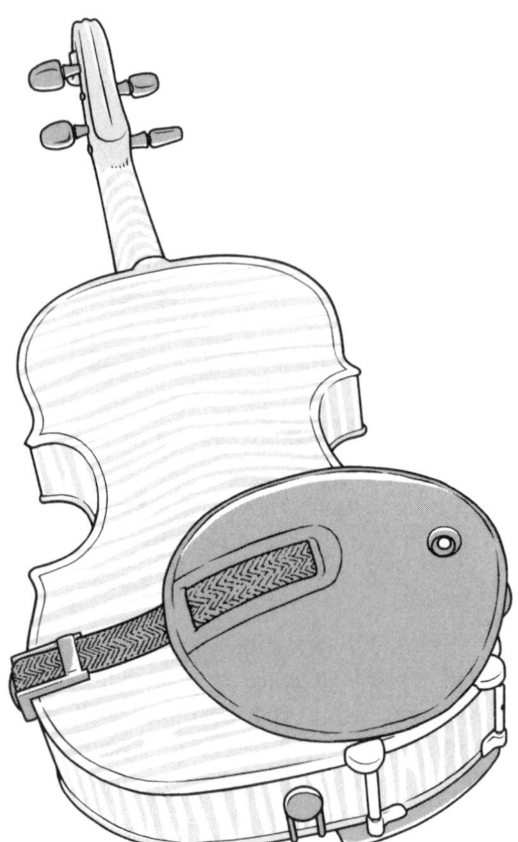

Damage

Note that the materials used for some pads or cushions can damage certain types of violin varnish. Sounds pretty vague indeed — so ask your violin maker or dealer for advice.

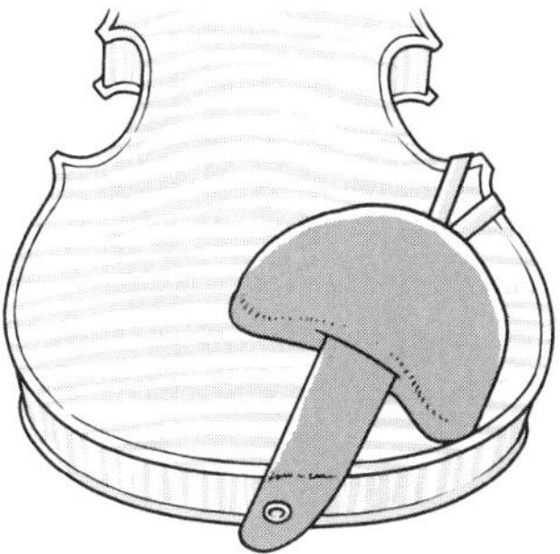

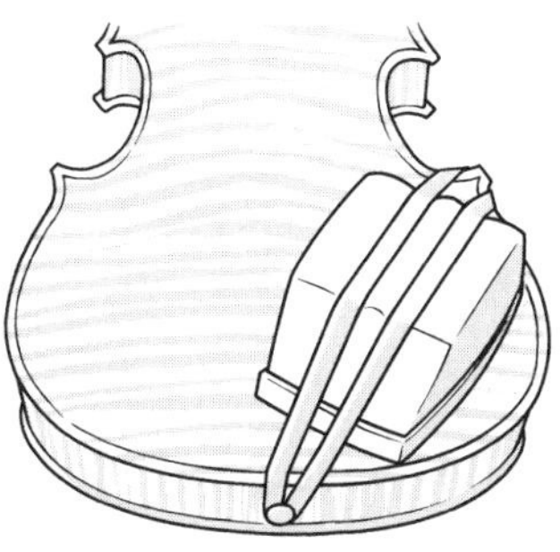

Cushions.

Bridge

Some violinists dislike pads or sponges, which they believe to muffle the vibrations of the back of the instrument. In reality, however, hardly anyone can really hear the difference. In case of doubt: There are pads that are mounted on a 'bridge,' so they don't touch the body of the violin. This also prevents damaging or wearing the varnish.

Fingers

The most popular shoulder rests consist of a wooden, plastic, or metal bar, covered with soft sponge rubber, which spans the back of the violin like a bridge. This type of shoulder rest is attached with four *fingers*. These should be adjustable so you can make the rest perfectly fit your instrument.

Tubing

A tip: Check now and again to see if the soft protective tubing of the fingers hasn't worn out, which would expose the finish and the wood of your violin to the metal underneath.

Height-adjustable

Some shoulder rests are also height-adjustable, on some the bar can be bent to perfectly fit your shoulders, and there are special shoulder rests available for musicians with wider or narrower shoulders. Non-adjustable models often come in two or more heights.

An adjustable shoulder rest.

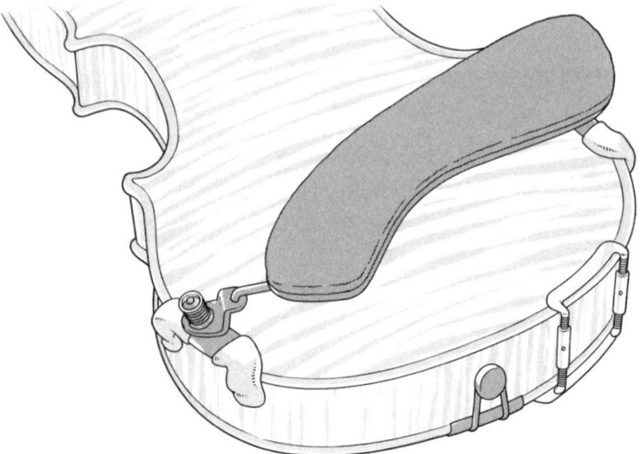

Attach and remove

When you're done playing, you need to take the shoulder rest off of your instrument. Some models are easier to attach and remove than others. *Tip:* Collapsible shoulder rests take up less space in your case.

Brands

Examples of well-known makers of shoulder rests are Johnson, Kadenza, Kun, Menuhin, Viva la Musica, and Wolf. Some brands offer shoulder rests in bright colors — red, blue, yellow — alongside their many models with a more traditional appearance. Fully adjustable shoulder rests are available from twenty or twenty-five dollars.

MUTES

If you place a *mute* on the bridge of your instrument, the sound becomes softer, mellower or warmer: Mutes muffle some of the higher frequencies of the sound. If the composer wants you to use a mute, the score will show the instruction 'with mute' in Italian: *con sordino*. Practice mutes (see page 23) muffle the sound a lot more than regular mutes do. A wolf tone eliminator (see below) is yet another type of mute, with a very specific purpose.

Clothing pin

As discussed on pages 48–51, a heavy bridge will slightly muffle the sound of your instrument. A mute works in pretty much the same way, as it simply adds mass to the bridge. The bigger or heavier a mute is, the more it will muffle the sound, the added mass absorbing the vibrations. Want to try it out? Very carefully attach a wooden clothing pin to the bridge of your instrument, and you'll hear that the sound will be muffled slightly. If you attach another clothing pin, doubling the added mass, the muffling effect will be even stronger.

TIP

> **Variety**
>
> ***Mutes come in rubber, metal, or wood, and in a wide variety of models. Most of them are very affordable, often costing under five dollars.***

Detachable or slide-on

The most basic mute, a three-pronged model, looks like a short, thick comb. You only put it onto your instrument when you need it. Another type, the *fixed mute* or *slide-on mute*, stays attached to your strings. If you don't need it, you slide it over toward the tailpiece. Slide-on mutes come in rubber (i.e., the Tourte model)

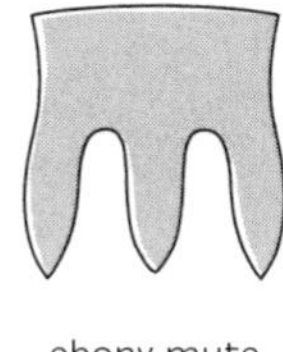

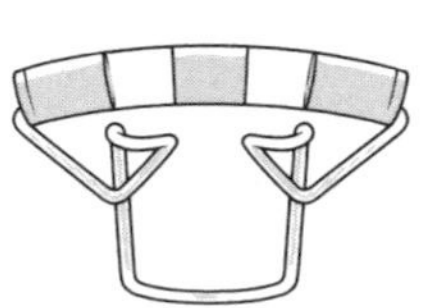

ebony mute | Tourte-style rubber mute | Hill model | slide-on wire mute

Different types of mutes

Which one

Slide-on mutes are especially easy if a composition requires you to alternately play with and without a mute. However, some players rather not use one because, even when it's at the tailpiece, a slide-on mute could muffle the sound (though you're unlikely to hear the difference), or because it might vibrate along with the strings, causing noise. Other musicians thoroughly dislike the other type of mutes (*clip-on mutes*) as they get lost so easily.

A tiny bit

A wire mute can be used to make your sound just a tiny bit sweeter. To do so, slide it to a position somewhere between

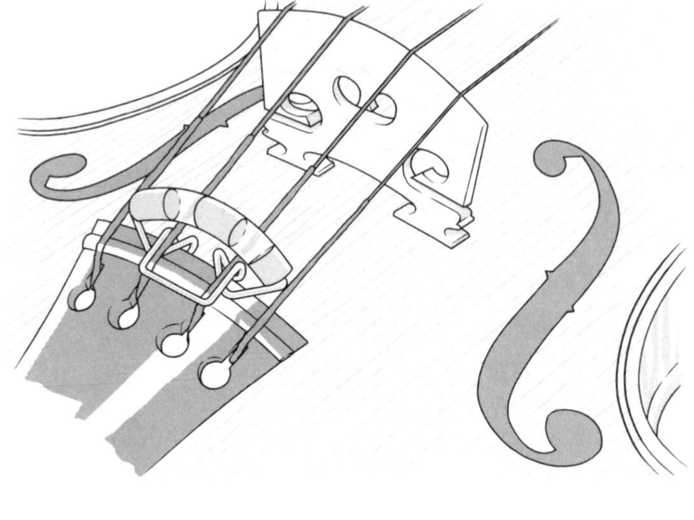

A slide-on wire mute at the tailpiece...

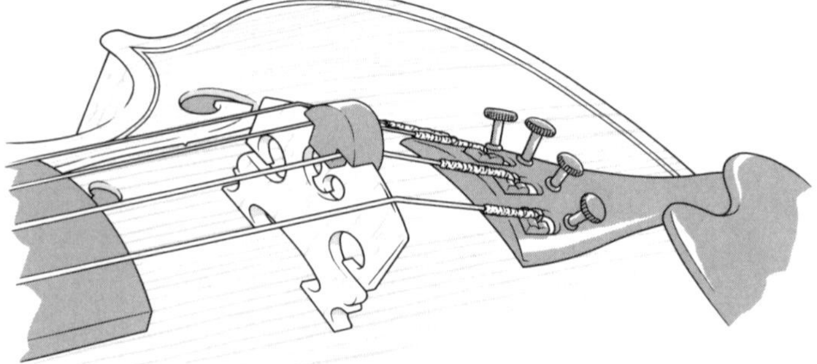

... and a rubber slide-on mute (Tourte) on the bridge.

the bridge and the tailpiece. The closer you get to the bridge, the stronger the muffling effect. You can also set a wire mute diagonally, so that it affects the high strings more than the low ones, or the other way around.

Wolf tone

Occasionally, a violin may produce a *wolf tone* — a stuttering sound, somewhat like a howling wolf. You can usually put an end to this problem with a *wolf tone eliminator*, a metal tube that is attached to the relevant string between bridge and tailpiece, wherever it has the greatest effect. Wolf tones are more common on cellos than on violins and violas.

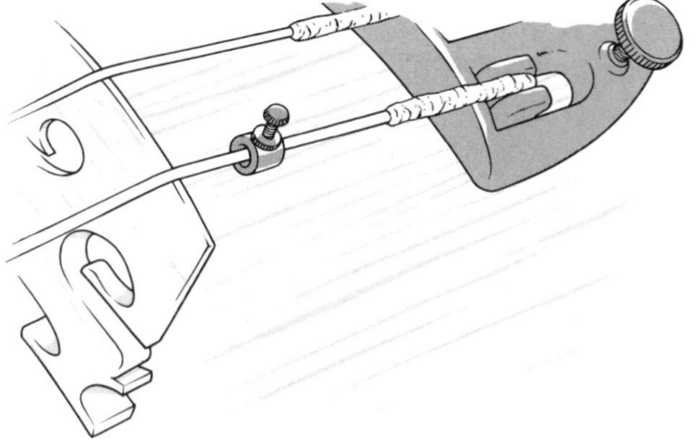

Wolf tone eliminator.

CASES

Except for low-budget instruments, violins and violas often come without a case — so usually you have to buy this essential protection separately.

Oblong or violin-shaped

Cases are available in a variety of styles. Oblong cases usually have one or more accessory pockets to store your shoulder rest, a set of spare strings, mutes, and rosin. *Shaped cases*, of which the outline vaguely resembles a violin, have less room for accessories.

Shell and covering

Most cases have a hard shell, made of plywood or plastic synthetic material (i.e., thermoplastic, ABS) covered with either vinyl, cloth, or leather.

Case covers

A violin case must be waterproof, so check that it really closes properly. Cases with a cloth, canvas, Cordura, or nylon cover often have a separate flap that goes across the opening. Separate

Case with backpack straps and extra storage space.

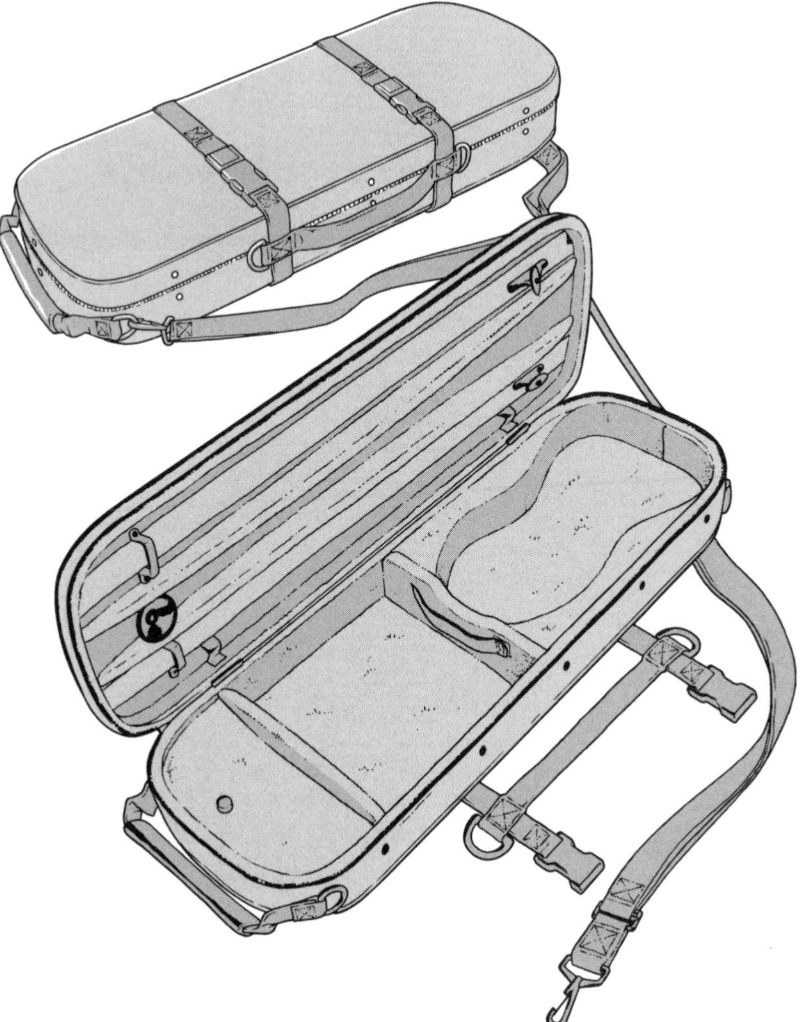

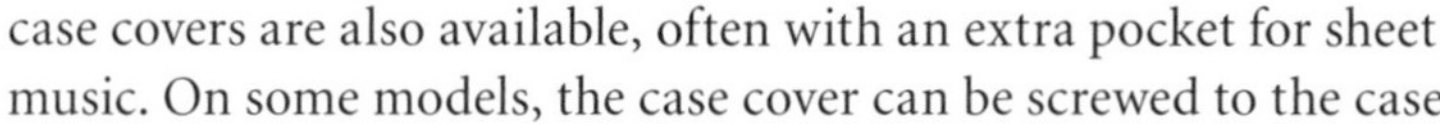

case covers are also available, often with an extra pocket for sheet music. On some models, the case cover can be screwed to the case.

Locks

Most cases are lockable. This is mainly to ensure that the catches cannot open by accident — for instance, if you drop the case — so make it a habit to always lock them.

Locks and hinges

When choosing a case, check the locks, hinges, handles, and carrying straps carefully. Usually, these are the weak spots.

A good case

A good case offers substantial shock absorption, and it's sturdy enough to resist being crushed as long as things don't get too extreme. The cheapest cases, with less padding and weaker cores, may not offer enough protection.

Two to six pounds

The lightest cases weigh only two pounds, whereas heavy models may weigh three times as much. Very light models are usually less shockproof than heavier ones. Incidentally, the violin itself weighs about a pound.

Inside

Many cases have a Velcro strip to hold the neck in place. It will also stop your violin from falling out, should you accidentally open the case the wrong way up. A case also should have a soft, plush-lined interior to absorb shocks and prevent scratches. The

Suspension cases

In many violin and viola cases, the instrument is suspended: The bottom is recessed at the back and the scroll of the instrument.

padding tends to be thicker in more expensive cases. If a choice between a velour or a velvet lining is offered, the latter will cost a little extra.

Bow holders

The inside of the lid usually has holders (*bow slots*) for two or sometimes three bows. A tip: Always put the bows in with their hair facing outwards. Separate bow cases are also available, for one or more bows.

Protective cloth

To prevent the bows from damaging or contaminating (rosin!) the instrument, cover the instrument with a cloth before closing the case. Some cases come with a cloth or a foam pad for that purpose. Instead of a cloth, you can use a bag. Many players prefer a silk one.

String tube

Cases always have room for spare strings. If you use gut strings, which should not be rolled up, you need a special *string tube.*

Backpack straps

If you don't drive, carrying your violin will be easier if your case has removable, adjustable backpack straps, or at least a shoulder strap.

Smaller and bigger

Because violas vary in size, viola cases come in different sizes too. The more expensive models are often adjustable. Some violin and viola cases come with a removable insert, so you can use the same case for instruments in various sizes. If you play violin as well as viola, you can get a case that holds both, and there are even cases that hold four instruments.

Prices

Expect to pay at least a hundred dollars for a case that can really take a knock, but you can get cheaper ones too, starting around fifty dollars. The most luxurious, leather-lined cases easily cost ten times as much.

TIP

Hygrometer

Violins are particularly sensitive to very dry air. Some of the more expensive cases available have a built-in hygrometer, so you can check humidity at any time (see pages 143–145).

Violin stands

If you take a short break, it may be easy to have a padded violin stand handy, rather than putting the violin back in its case or laying it down somewhere. Violin stands, available for less than twenty dollars, usually have a holder for the bow too. They're typically foldable. Setting up is a matter of seconds.

C-Bout Protector

To prevent your bow from hitting the C-bout of your violin — which may damage one or the other — you may install a C-bout protector, a soft plastic device that easily clips onto the instrument.

9

Electric Violins

If you play your violin in a band, you're likely to find that it isn't loud enough. Rather than use a regular microphone, you can get yourself a ready-made electric violin, or turn your classical instrument into an electric one, or attach a clip-on microphone to it. Electric violins can also be used to practice in complete silence, using headphones.

Basically, there are two types of electric violins: The ones that hardly produce any sound at all when unamplified, and regular violins that have been converted to electric ones. The latter can be played unamplified (i.e., acoustically) as well, so they're really acoustic/electric instruments.

Acoustic/electric violins

Converting a regular violin to an electric one is a matter of mounting one or two *pickups* or *transducers*. These small, flat 'sensors' literally pick up the vibrations of the strings, and convert them to electric signals that can be amplified.

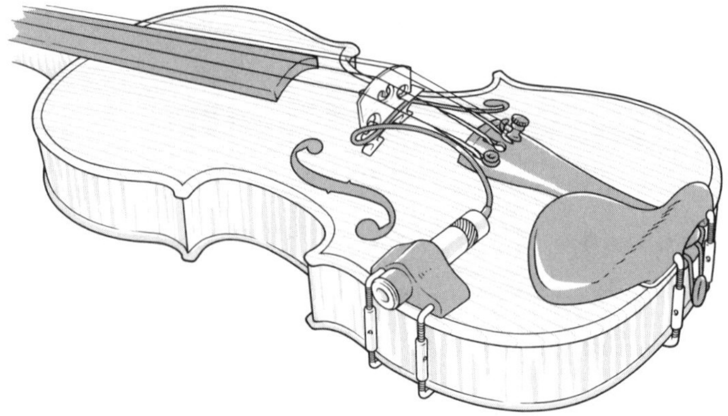

Acoustic/electric violin with a pickup in the bridge.

Between wings and feet

Most violin pickups are wedged between the bridge wings and feet, or under the feet. Because your bridge will usually need some filing for a good fit, and because the precise positioning is very important to the sound, it's best to let an expert install them for you. Alternatively, you can get a pickup that sticks to the bridge with adhesive.

Preamplifier

The signals produced by most pickups need to be boosted before they're sent to the main amplifier. In ready-made electric violins, the required preamplifier is usually built into the instrument, and so are its controls (e.g., volume and tone). If you install a pickup on a regular violin, you can attach the preamp to your clothing or your belt. Also, there are systems that have their controls in a chin rest style device.

Output

The output for the instrument cable is usually mounted on the side of the instrument, or on its tailpiece. Some systems have a standard ¼" phone jack output; others use a smaller (3.5 mm), lighter mini jack.

Feedback

Using pickups, you can play really loud without too much risk of being bothered by feedback — the loud screech you also hear if you point a microphone at a loudspeaker. However, pickups can make your instrument sound less warm and natural than a microphone would.

Clip-on microphone

That's why some violinists prefer to use a miniature clip-on microphone — which has the drawback of making the instrument more sensitive to feedback. Clip-on microphones need a preamp too.

Both worlds

A best-of-both-worlds solution is to use a pickup as well as a (vocal) microphone on a stand, or to buy a set that features both a pickup and a clip-on microphone. Such systems feature a control to set the balance between the two. You use just the microphone if timbre is what counts and the required volume is low enough not to cause feedback, or just the pickup if you're playing with a really loud band, or a well-balanced mix of the two. Yet another alternative is a bridge-mounted microphone that has the sound characteristics of a microphone but looks like a pickup, and behaves like a pickup when it comes to resisting feedback.

Cotton wool or notch filter

Even when using pickups on your 'regular' violin, feedback can occur. A basic trick to fight feedback is to fill the body of your instrument with bits of cotton wool, which can later be removed

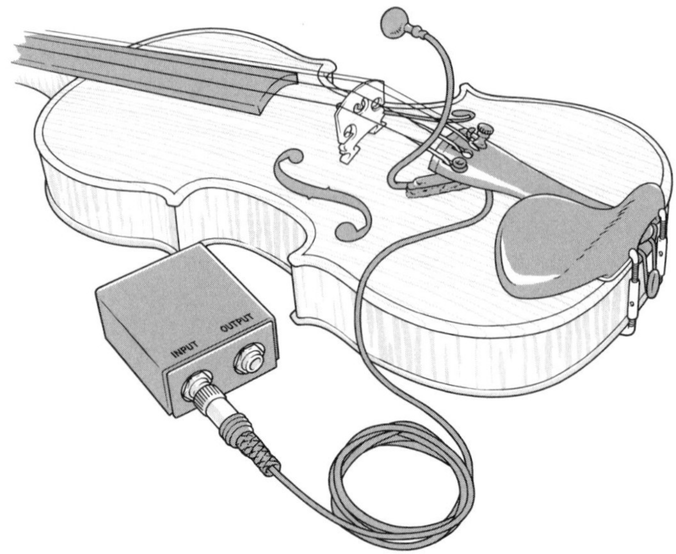

A clip-on microphone and a preamp (SD Systems).

with a crotchet needle. (Take care not to touch the sound post!) A more sophisticated solution is to use a (pre)amp with a *notch filter*, which combats feedback by filtering the offending frequency out of the sound. A *phase switch* can also help to fight feedback.

Prices and brands

You can buy a decent violin pickup for as little as seventy-five dollars, and sometimes even less, but you can spend a lot more too: Systems with both a pickup and a microphone can easily set you back some five hundred dollars. Some well-known companies in this field include Barcus Berry, B-band, Bowtronics, Fishman, L.R. Baggs, Schaller, SD Systems, Seymour Duncan, and Shadow.

Solid-body violins

Solid-body electric violins — which are designed to be played 'electric only' — come in many different shapes. Some still have the basic outline of the traditional instrument; others have solid bodies in Z-, S-, V-shaped or other designs.

Frets and seven strings

These instruments feature all sorts of other options as well. For example, there are electric violins with a fretted neck (like a

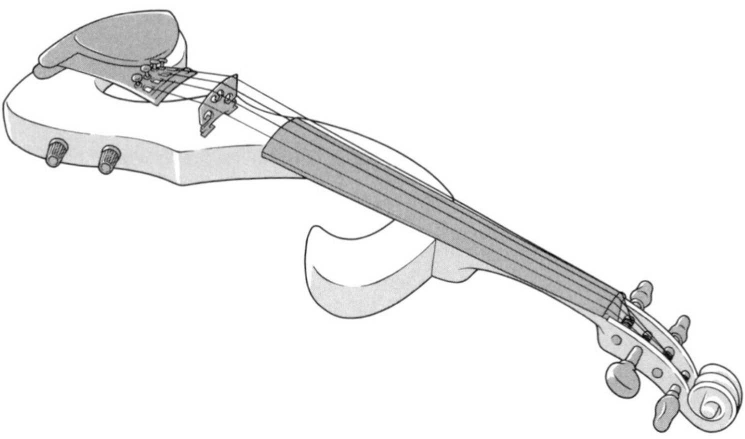

Electric violin (Straus).

guitar), and you can get them with five, six or seven strings. The extra strings are all tuned to lower pitches than the regular violin's G. Five-string acoustic/electric violins are available too.

Silence

Solid-body electric violins can of course be used for silent practice as well. The best-known example of an instrument that was designed specifically for that purpose is Yamaha's Silent Violin (see page 24). It features a small built-in amplifier for a pair of headphones, and there's an input to connect an MP3 player or another playback device to the instrument, allowing you to play along with pre-recorded music. Also, it has a built-in reverb to add some extra life to the sound. Of course, the instrument can be amplified as well.

Prices and brands

Electric violins are available from around three hundred to more than three thousand dollars. Some of the companies that make solid-body violins are T.F. Barrett, Bridge, Fender (the guitar makers), Fidelius, Jensen, Jordan, NS (Ned Steinberger), Skyinbow, Stagg, Starfish, Straus, TB, Violectra, Wood, and Zeta. Ready-made acoustic/electric instruments are available from Barcus-Berry, Importuno, Meisel, Palatino, Phoenix, and others. Some of these companies focus on budget instruments; others offer professional violins only, or a wider range of instruments.

Midi

Some electric violins can be hooked up to synthesizers, effect devices, computers, and other digital equipment. For this purpose, they feature midi, a standardized musical instrument digital interface.

Amplification

If you play electric, you can either use the band's or the venue's PA system, or you can buy your own amplifier. Most violinists use a special type of amp that is designed to be used for acoustic instruments, known as — believe it or not — an *acoustic amplifier.* They're usually combo amplifiers, with one or more relatively small loudspeakers and an amplifier all in one box, often featuring one or more effects such as reverb or chorus. Some players prefer a regular guitar amp (designed for electric guitars) instead. For more information, please check out *Tipbook Amplifiers and Effects* (See *The Tipbook Series*, page 223).

10

Tuning

A violin has to be tuned before you can play it. When you start out your teacher will tune it for you, but sooner or later you'll have to do it yourself. Is it difficult? No, not really – but it does take a lot of practice. This chapter offers basic information and helpful hints.

A violin won't easily go out of tune if it's in good condition. Even so, you always need to check its tuning before you start playing, and it can't hurt to check the tuning from time to time while you are playing.

Tuning pegs

It is hard to tune synthetic strings and — even more so — steel strings with the tuning pegs only. Even the slightest rotation of a peg translates into a major pitch difference. If you're not careful, you even can easily tighten a string so much that it breaks.

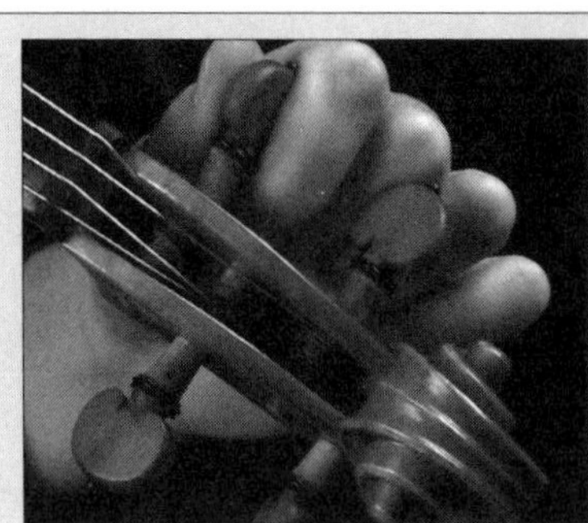

Tipcode VIOLIN-008

Even the slightest rotation of a peg translates into a major pitch difference.

Fine tuners

That's why synthetic and steel strings usually have fine tuners. The large wooden tuning pegs are used only to roughly 'pretune' the strings. When you do so, always make sure the fine tuners are in their middle settings. This allows you to use them to tune the strings up as well as down.

Tuning as you bow...

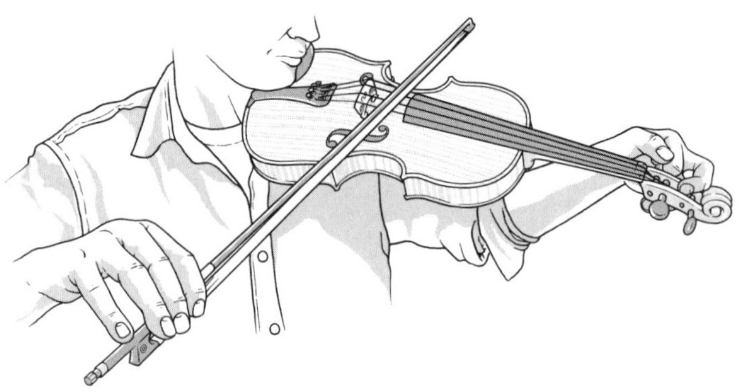

Plucking or bowing?

You can sound the string you are tuning by plucking, as you would with a guitar. For beginners, plucking is easiest — but bowing the strings allows you to hear the strings' pitches easier. Before you can do either, you'll have to learn how to hold your violin under your chin while you bow or pluck with your right hand, and operate the fine tuners or pegs with your left.

The pitches

The strings of a violin and viola are tuned to the following pitches:

	Violin	Viola
String 1	E5	A4 (thinnest, highest sounding string)
String 2	A4	D4
String 3	D4	G3
String 4	G3	C3 (thickest, lowest sounding string)

The A

Most orchestral instruments are tuned to the A that sounds the same pitch as the A-string of a well-tuned violin or viola.

A=440

If a string sounds at this pitch, it vibrates 440 times per second. This pitch is usually referred to as A=440 hertz or simply A=440.

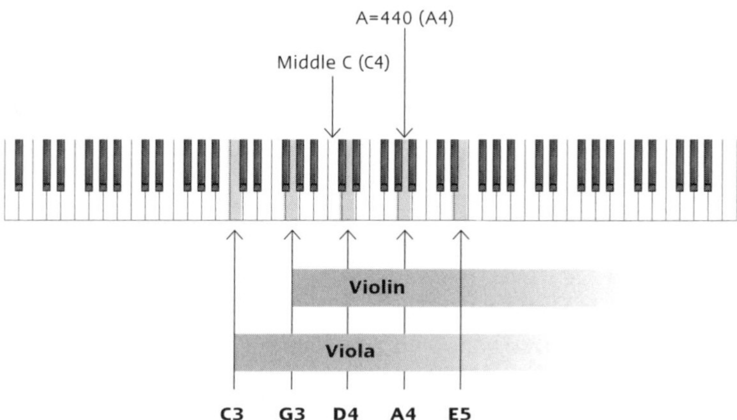

Oboe

In an orchestra, the oboe plays this note, and all musicians tune their instruments to it. If you're by yourself, you can make A=440 sound using a tuning fork, a piano, an electronic tuner, or Tipcode Violin-009, for example.

Tuning fork

A tuning fork is a thick, two-pronged metal fork that sounds a reference pitch, typically A=440. Simply tap the fork on your knee, hold the stem against or near your ear, and you'll hear this A.

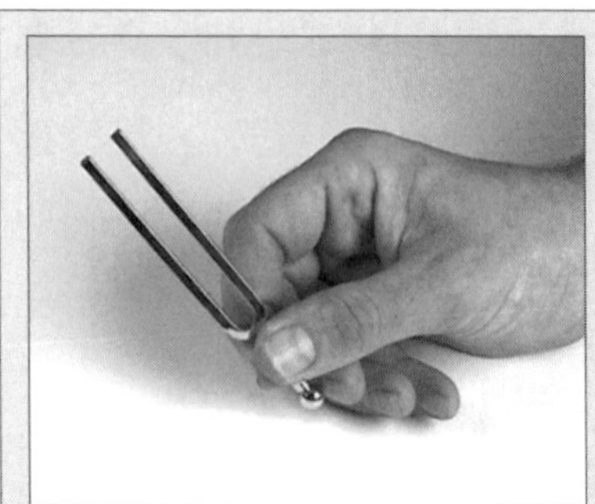

Tipcode VIOLIN-009

As you can see in this Tipcode, you can also tap a tuning fork on a table top and use the table as a soundboard to amplify the sound.

A=442

Some orchestras tune to an A that is a tiny bit higher. You can buy tuning forks for these tunings too, such as A=442. Tuning forks sell for some five to fifteen dollars.

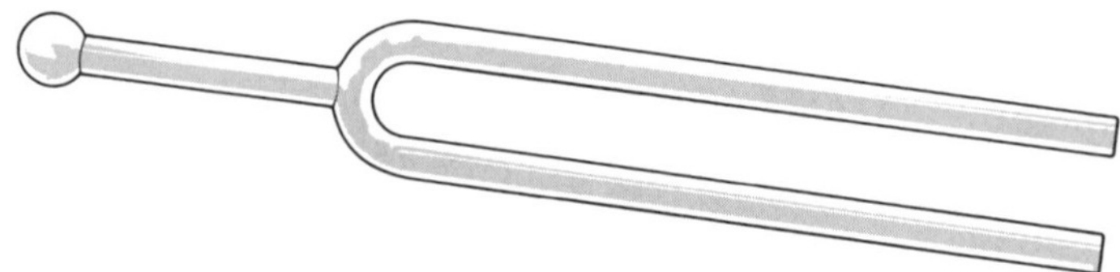

Tuning fork.

Metronomes and tuners

A=440 can be played back on many electronic metronomes and electronic tuners as well. There's more on electronic tuners on page 120–121.

Piano

If you have a piano around, you can match the pitch of your A string to the corresponding note on the piano. This is the A to the right of Middle C, typically indicated as A4 (see page 115): it's the A in the piano's fourth octave.

Pedal

If you use a piano, press the right pedal down and then play this A-key. This will make the note sound for a long time, which makes it easier to use for reference as you tune your violin. Do note that the piano should be perfectly in tune!

Too high, too low?

The first string you tune is always the A. Listen to the reference pitch A and turn the fine tuner until the string sounds that same pitch. In the beginning, it can be difficult to hear whether a string is too high (*sharp*) or too low (*flat*). Here's a trick: First turn the fine tuner of the relevant string all the way down. Then you can be almost certain that its pitch is flat. From there, slowly bring the string up to the right pitch.

Tipcode VIOLIN-006

Tuning up (rather than down) to the required pitch, as demonstrated in this clip, usually works best.

Singing

You can also sing along. First listen closely to the reference pitch and sing it. Then sing the pitch the string is making. Usually, you will then 'feel' if you have to sing higher or lower, and you can adjust the string accordingly.

Tipcode VIOLIN-010

This Tipcode demonstrates the pitch differences between the strings.

In the middle

If you start with the fine tuners in their middle settings, you can typically tune each string up or down a whole step or even more. In most cases, this is enough to get them to the correct pitches.

The E

Once the A is right, tune the E-string. You can find this E on a piano too (E5), but you can also do it without one. Try singing the first two words of *Twinkle, Twinkle, Little Star.* If you sing the first *Twinkle* at the same pitch as your A-string, the second *Twinkle* will be at the pitch your E-string should have.

Perfect fifth

The 'distance' or *interval* from the first to the second *Twinkle* is referred to as a *perfect fifth.*

Backwards

On violins and violas, all adjacent strings are a perfect fifth apart. To tune a lower sounding string to a higher sounding string, you should sing the first two 'Twinkles' backwards: Sing the second, higher sounding *Twinkle* while playing the higher sounding string, and match the lower sounding string to the first, lower sounding *Twinkle.*

G and D

This way, you can tune the D-string to the A-string, and then tune the G to the D.

Viola

On a viola you also begin with the A-string, of course. From there go to the D, the G, and finally the C. The interval between each pair of strings, again, is a perfect fifth.

Check

When you have tuned all four strings, check them once more. Usually you'll have to adjust the tuning here or there. The nursery rhyme will point you in the right direction, but there is a better way to hear whether the instrument is in perfect tune.

Better still

The trick is to bow two adjacent strings. Again, a perfectly tuned A string is your reference. If the sound of any pair of strings is slightly wavy, carefully adjust the second string. The slower the waves or 'beats' get, the closer you are. When they're gone, the string pair is in tune, so proceed to the next pair.

Tipcode VIOLIN-013
Bowing adjacent strings is of great help when tuning your instrument.

Harmonics

Another way to check your tuning is by using harmonics. Tune your A-string. Now touch it very lightly at exactly one third of its length and bow it. The tone you will hear now is known as a *harmonic*. This harmonic sounds an octave above the pitch of your E-string. To compare the two strings, play the harmonic at one third of the A-string and the harmonic that you get when lightly touching the E-string exactly in the middle. Adjust the (fine tuner of the) E-string if the pitches don't match exactly.
Next, play the harmonic of the D-string at one third and of the

A-string half way (adjust the D-string to match the A-string). Do the same for the G and the D string — and finally, check the overall tuning once more before you start playing.

Reference pitches

You can also tune your instrument by tuning each string to a reference pitch. You can do so with a piano (the keys to play are shown on page 115), with the reference pitches of Tipcodes below, or with an electronic tuner (see below). Still, it's better to learn to tune your violin or viola with nothing more than an A=440 as a reference pitch. After all, that's how you'll often have to do it if you play in an orchestra or in another group or ensemble.

Tipcode VIOLIN-011 and VIOLIN-012

Reference pitches for violin strings are played in Tipcode Violin-011. For viola string pitches, check out Tipcode Violin-012.

Careful

If you are adjusting your fine tuners as you bow, there's a good chance you'll press them down slightly without meaning to. This pressure will make the string's pitch go up. So as soon as you let go of the fine tuner, the pitch will drop, and you'll have to start again. The solution? First adjust the string, then let go of the fine tuner and listen — and so on.

Bowing

When you're tuning, try to make sure you bow with a consistent, light pressure. If you don't, the tuning may turn out to be less than perfect as soon as you start playing.

Chromatic tuner

A chromatic electronic *tuner* tells you exactly which pitch it is hearing, and whether it is flat, *sharp*, or exactly right. Simply play and adjust your strings one by one. Prices for this type of tuner start at some twenty-five dollars. These tuners are especially popular with guitarists and (electric) bassists, but string players can use them too. That said, you will often hear that it's better to learn to tune by ear. This helps you develop your sense of pitch — and you need that more than guitarists, who play fretted instruments.

A chromatic tuner.

A little higher

Strings stretch as they get older. Eventually they may come to a point where your fine tuners can't get them in tune anymore. If so, you'll have to tune them a little higher with your pegs. Before you

> ***Vibrational tuners***
>
> *Chromatic tuners have a built-in microphone that picks up the frequency of the string you're playing. It also 'hears' all your fellow orchestra members tune. The solution is a vibrational tuner, which you simply clip onto your instrument. It uses a vibration sensor to pick up the vibrations (i.e. the frequency) of the string you play. There's no microphone, so it can't pick up the sound of the instruments that are being played or tuned around you.*

do, first loosen the string with the fine tuner as far as it will go. *Tip:* If a string has been stretched this far, chances are it needs to be replaced.

Tuning with pegs

When you use the pegs, it's easiest if you tune upwards. So if a string sounds sharp, first turn the peg until the pitch is clearly too low; then go back up from there. Apart from that, tuning with pegs is really the same as tuning with fine tuners — though it may take some time to learn how to adjust them.

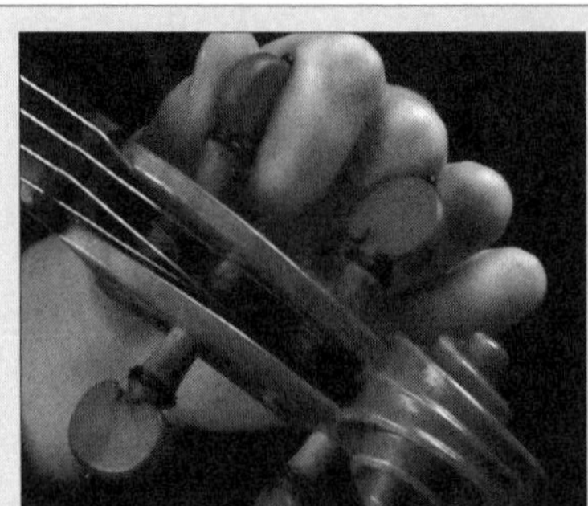

Tipcode VIOLIN-008
First tune down, then tune up to the required pitch.

Additional tuning tips

- Important: Always turn the tuning pegs **very slowly** and no more than a little at a time.
- After some practice, you will know **which peg to turn** for each string. To find the correct one, simply follow the string you want to tune into the peg box. It's easy to remember that the peg for the A-string is the upper one.
- New strings detune easily. You can take some of the slack out by gently **stretching them**, pulling them away from the fingerboard. You will find that this makes the pitch drop, so carefully tune them up again.
- Adjusting the pitch of one string will change the tension on — and therefore the pitch of — **all other strings**, so always check the overall tuning of the instrument after each adjustment.

- **Pitch pipes** are inexpensive, but they tend to go out of tune quickly, so many violinists prefer to use a tuning fork.

Scordatura

Very occasionally, violins are tuned to different pitches. For example, the pitch of the lowest string might be tuned down a half or a whole step. Such alternative tunings are known as *scordatura*.

11

Violin Maintenance

Violin repairs and adjustments are best left to an expert. But there is plenty you can do yourself to keep your instrument in the best possible condition: cleaning, replacing strings, straightening the bridge, and more.

The rosin from your bow lands on your violin as dust. You can easily wipe most of it off with a soft, lint-free cloth each time you finish playing. A cotton cloth will do fine; an old, unprinted T-shirt for instance, or a dishcloth. Watch out for splinters around the edges, especially with older instruments. On some finishes (e.g., synthetic finishes) you can use a slightly damp cloth as well, if necessary. *Tip:* Don't forget to wipe the bow stick too.

Fingerboard and strings

It's best to use a different cloth for the neck, strings, and fingerboard, where you touch them with your fingers. Wipe the strings with the cloth and then pull it between the fingerboard and the strings. Again, a cotton cloth is good for the job, but some violinists prefer to use silk. Once you've wiped your violin, put it back in its case.

Prevention

Strings will live longer if you wash your hands before playing, and your violin will be easier to keep clean if you only hold it by the neck and in the chin rest area.

Violin cleaner

Every violin needs extra attention once in a while, even if you are very careful. The top can get sticky and dull, especially between the *f*-holes, where most of the rosin ends up. You can remove it with a special violin cleaner.

Violin polish

There are special cleaners and cleaning cloths that polish your instrument as well, smoothing away fine scratches.

The best?

Which is the best cleaner for your violin depends on its varnish, so always ask what you can and cannot use on your instrument when you buy or rent it. Before using a cleaner, always read the instructions. Then try a small area first, preferably one that's out

of sight. Some delicate varnishes may be damaged by an abrasive polish, or by a cleaner that contains harsh solvents.

Never

Whatever you do, never use ordinary household cleaners. One exception would be using a window cleaner on a plastic chin rest. Do take the chin rest off first.

The fingerboard

You can occasionally give the fingerboard an extra cleaning by dabbing it with a soft cloth, moistened with some rubbing alcohol. Make sure that no liquid gets onto the varnish of the body of the instrument. Keep the bottle well out of the way and do not allow the cloth to drag over the body. For safety's sake, lay another dry cloth over the body.

The strings

Your strings need to be cleaned from time to time, removing rosin residue, grime, and finger oils. Take a clean cloth and push it along the strings a few times from the top of the fingerboard to the bridge. Don't push too hard, and hold one hand across the strings, because they can really screech when you do this.

Alcohol, steel wool, and string oil

If this doesn't work, you may moisten the cloth with rubbing alcohol, provided you don't use gut strings. Again, do not spill any of this liquid on the instrument. Special string cleaners are available as well, including biologically degradable, solvent-free cleaners. Two more tips:

- Some technicians use very **fine grade steel wool** (0000) to remove rosin residue.
- Plain gut strings retain their elasticity by treating them with special **string oil** or almond oil.

Inside

Over the years, dust and dirt will inevitably find their way into your violin or viola. Some players clean the inside of their instruments by pouring a handful of dry, uncooked rice through the *f*-holes and gently shaking the body around a few times. Then they turn the instrument upside down and shake it some more. This procedure cleans the underside of the top. As the rice pours out of the f-holes, it will automatically take along most of the dust from the inside.

Rattles

If you use this technique, though, there's always a risk that a grain will get caught inside (in a tiny gap between the lining and the side, for example) and cause rattling, especially in instruments that are roughly made or have been frequently repaired.

Check

You should regularly inspect your violin for splinters or other minor damage. Also check whether the chin rest is still secure, and that the tubing of the fingers of your shoulder rest is in good shape.

Expert

There are times when you'll need to take your instrument to an expert — when it needs more extensive cleaning, if there are stains that won't go away, if you can't get the neck clean, or if the varnish is becoming very dull (on the body, under the strings, or where you touch the body with your left hand). Many musicians have their instruments checked once a year by a violin maker or technician, even if nothing seems to be wrong, just to be on the safe side.

Plastic

If your perspiration is especially acidic, it can damage the varnish and even the wood of the ribs where your left hand touches it. The solution? There are violin makers who simply stick a strip of self-adhesive plastic to the instrument. Others makers are appalled at the very idea of sticking plastic to a violin. As an alternative, you can try using a cloth or velvet bib.

TUNING PEGS

Fine tuners do not require much maintenance, if any at all. If one does get a little stiff, you may apply a tiny bit of acid-free Vaseline. Wooden tuning pegs, on the other hand, can be troublesome.

Peg compound

The tuning pegs need to be able to turn smoothly, without slipping back. If they get stuck or they slip, try using a little peg compound or peg dope. Other players prefer tailor's chalk, also known as French or Venetian chalk. If these treatments aren't effective anymore, you can clean the peg and peg hole with a little benzene.

Stopgap solutions

A stopgap solution for a slipping peg is to apply a bit of saliva to it. White chalk will help too, but it will also make the hole wear out faster. Some players use soap, but soap may congeal and make tuning harder. Another alternative is to wind your strings so that they force the peg deeper into the peg hole, by letting the string wind up against the cheek of the peg box. This too is a stopgap solution: Jamming the string against the cheek may cause it to break (see page 137).

Loose

If a peg or its hole is badly worn, the peg may get really loose. Having a new set of bigger pegs custom-fit to the instrument will usually cost some fifty to a hundred dollars. This may or may not include the pegs, which typically vary from ten to fifty dollars for a

Compound, dope, drops

There's quite some confusion when it comes to the names of peg compound, peg drops, and so on. Some say that peg compound cures both sticky and slipping pegs; others use peg compound for the substance that cures sticky pegs only, using peg drops to remedy slipping pegs.

set — but there are more expensive ones too, with golden rings or other expensive decorations. If the peg holes are really worn out, they can be *rebushed*.

BOW

Maintaining your bow comes down to applying rosin to it, keeping it clean and having it rehaired when necessary. Here are some helpful hints.

Rosin

Applying rosin is necessary only when the bow hair gets too smooth, probably no more than once or twice a week. Move the bow hair over the rosin cake rather than the other way around, applying the rosin along the full length of the hair, from the head to the frog. If you keep your thumb on the ferrule when you do this, it won't damage the rosin cake.

Two tips

Here are some extra helpful tips:

- **Rotate the cake** in order to prevent the bow hair from wearing a groove in it, creating 'walls' of unusable rosin.
- **Don't touch** the bow hair or the cake with your fingers, as perspiration and finger oil will keep the rosin from holding on to the bow hair.
- Does your bow need rosin? Slide the bow hair over a dark cloth. If this leaves a **white mark**, things are fine. No traces? Then get your rosin out.

Excess rosin

Wipe the bow hair with a cloth when you have finished, or drag one of your nails across the bow hairs close to the frog. This makes sure that the excess rosin doesn't land on your violin. You can shake out your bow instead, but it's best not to. Even if you don't break anything or hit anybody, whipping can damage your bow.

Tipcode VIOLIN-014

This video show you how to move the bow hair over the rosin cake, rather than the other way around.

Cleaning

The bow hair often gets a bit grimy near the frog. You can clean this with a damp cloth. (Perhaps apply a drop of dishwashing liquid to the lukewarm water.) *Tip:* The ends of the bow hair are held in place by small wooden wedges. Make sure not to get them wet.

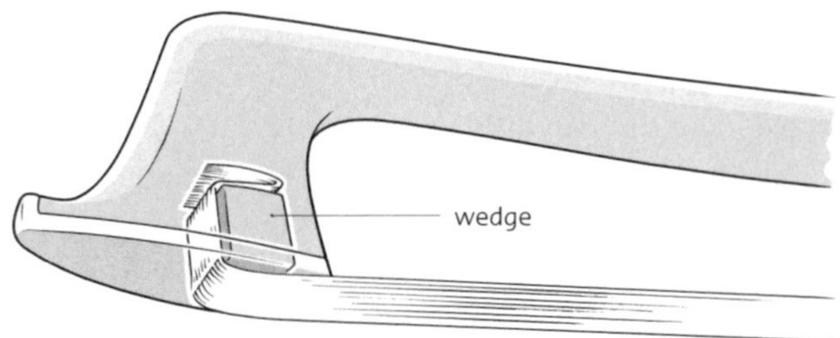

The bow hair is held in place by small wooden wedges.

Too smooth

If you need to apply rosin more and more often, that's probably due to old bow hair (have it replaced) or to a buildup of rosin residue, which makes the hair slick. Some violinists clean the hair themselves, using a cloth that's very lightly moistened with rubbing alcohol — but it is much safer to have it done by an expert.

The liquid may damage the stick, and you may end up with the bow hair sticking together, rendering the bow unplayable. A bow maker or violin technician can decide whether cleaning will help, or if a rehair is required.

New hair

If the bow hair is overstretched, you can't get the bow back to proper tension. The usual solution is a rehair. A rehair typically costs some forty or fifty dollars. In some cases, the bow hair can be shortened instead.
If you only play for a few hours a week, the bow hair will typically last for about three years

Broken bow hair

If a hair breaks, remove the loose ends by cutting them off at the sharp edge of the ferrule and the face, rather than pulling them out. Another solution is to cut them carefully with scissors, as close as possible to the ferrule and the face.

Not tight

If you can't get the hair to the desired tension, the bow hair may be overstretched, or your bow stick could be slowly losing its curvature. A bow maker or violin technician may be able to restore this.

Slide smoothly

If the frog doesn't slide smoothly and the end screw feels stiff, remove them by turning the end screw until it comes off. A simple cleaning will usually do. Don't use oil for screw parts. Instead, gently rub the screw on a candle. If this doesn't solve the problem, then have the bow looked after. Do so too if the frog wobbles or if the grip needs to be replaced.

NEW STRINGS

You need to replace strings if they break, if their windings comes loose, or when they get older. The older strings get, the harder it will be to tune them, and their sound gets noticeably duller. The better your violin is, the better your play, and the better your ears and your sense of pitch, the sooner you'll notice when strings need to be replaced.

How long

How long a set of strings will last you depends on many things. If you have synthetic strings and you play for a few hours a week, you might try fitting new strings after six months or so. If you hear the difference straightaway, try replacing the new set after just four months. If you can't hear any difference after six months, wait a little longer before replacing your strings next time. Your strings will always last you longer if you keep your strings and your hands clean, and if your perspiration isn't too acidic.

When to replace strings

Steel strings usually last a bit longer than synthetic strings, and gut strings wear out the quickest. When should you replace your strings? When plucking them only produces a short, dull tone, it's a sign that they are wearing out. If they become discolored, you're also better off replacing them. Note, however, that silver-wound strings may still sound fine long after they have begun to discolor.

Wound strings

Some windings — aluminum, for instance — are easily blemished by certain types of perspiration. If this happens, try using a set of strings with a different type of winding, such as chrome-steel. Different strings will not sound the same, of course — so you may need to compromise: the sound you're after, or strings that last longer…

A new set

If one of your wound strings breaks, the new string you put on may sound a lot brighter than the older ones. If so, the only solution is to replace the other wound strings too. A new E-string can usually be fitted without replacing the rest. Some violinists claim their instrument sounds better if they use cheap E-strings and replace them often, rather than playing one expensive E-string for a longer period of time. A tip: Used strings can still be useful as spares.

Not more than two

Before replacing your strings, lay your violin on a folded towel, or on your lap. An important tip: Don't take off more than two strings at a time, so that the other strings keep the bridge and sound post in place. If the sound post still falls over, loosen all the strings and have the post set in position by an expert.

Tipcode VIOLIN-015

How to remove a string is shown in this Tipcode Violin.

Removing strings

To remove a string, slightly pull the peg outward and slowly turn it toward the body of the instrument. Then pull gently on the string, so the peg will start turning until the string comes loose. Guide the string between your thumb and index finger near the pegbox, so that it can't suddenly come loose and cause damage.

Cut

You can also turn the peg until the string is slack and then cut it by the pegbox. It is easier and safer to remove the remaining bit than a whole, long string, some say.

Fitting strings

You can fit new strings in various ways. This is one simple way.

- Turn the peg so that the hole points diagonally upwards, facing the fingerboard.
- Attach the string to the tailpiece.
- Stick the string through the peg (illustration 1) and start winding it. Make sure the hole moves in the direction of the scroll.

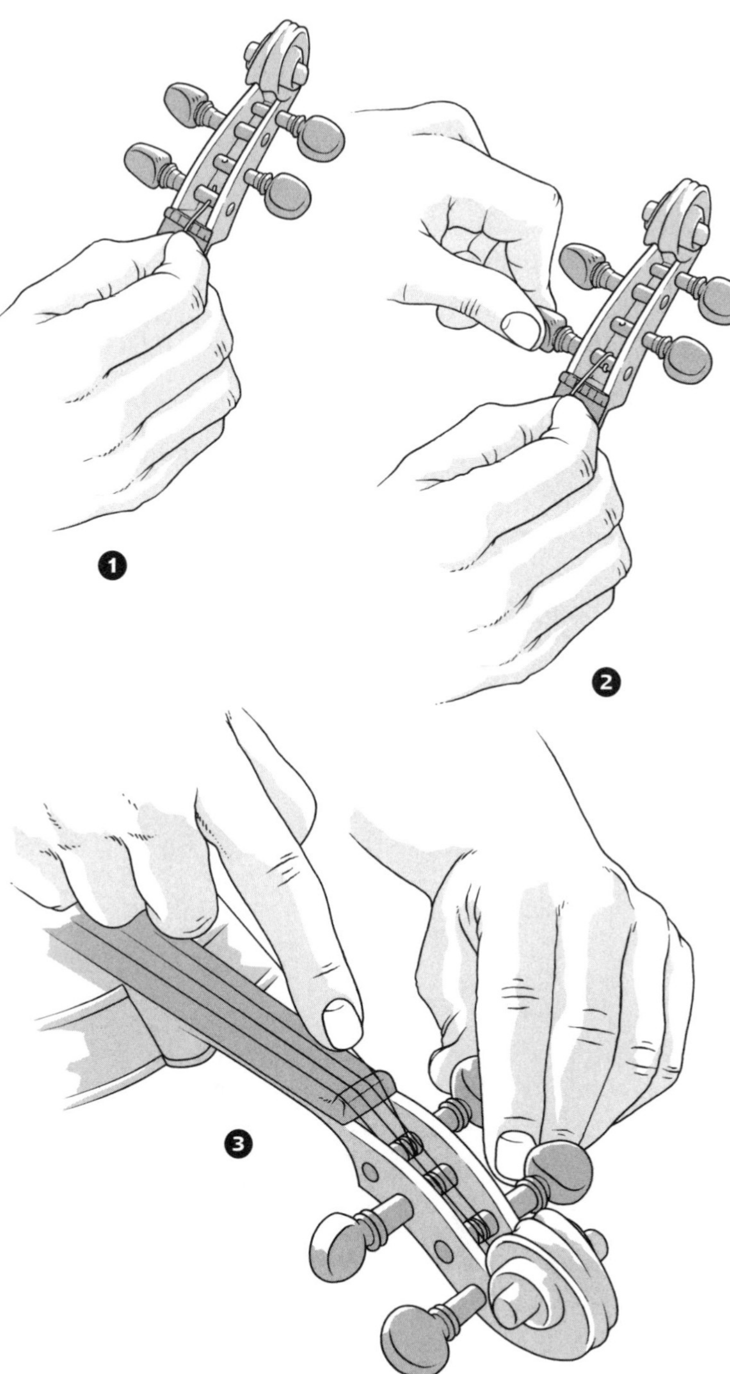

Fitting a new string.

- Hold the string with your other hand so that it can't go slack and slip out of the hole or come loose from the tailpiece (illustration 2).
- Keep tightening the string, making sure that the windings run outwards, toward the thicker end of the peg. Use your index finger to keep the string tight and to guide it through the groove in the nut (illustration 3).
- Tune it so that it is at roughly the right tension (using the corresponding peg), comparing it to the strings that are still in place.

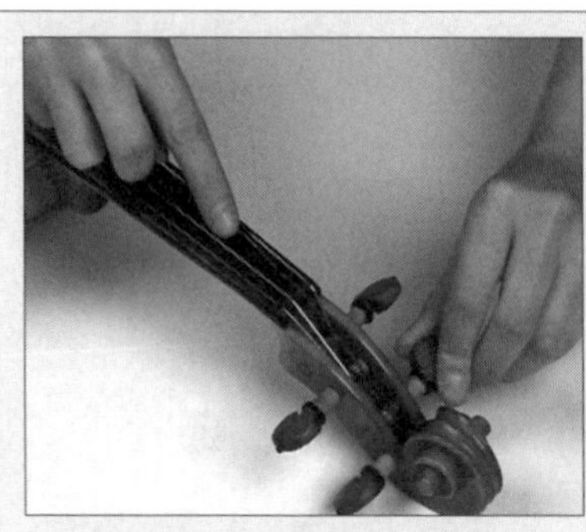

Tipcode VIOLIN-016

This Tipcode shows you how to fit a new string.

This way, the strings will always stay properly in place. Make a kink in the string, lay it against the peg, and let the unwound part of the string wind around it a couple of times.

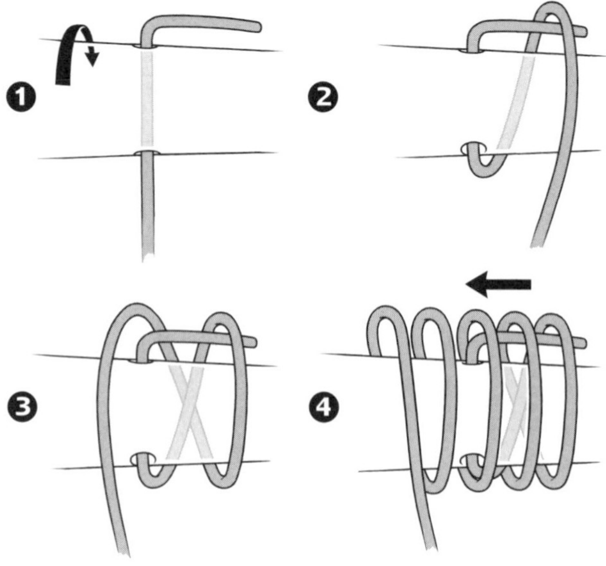

Kink

You may find that a string keeps on coming loose from the peg as you try to tighten it. If so, take a small pair of pliers and make a kink about half an inch (1–1.5 cm) from the very end of the string. The kink will make the string hook itself in place as you begin to turn the peg.

Pegs in poor condition

Similar kinks can also help keep strings in place if your pegs are in poor condition. Stick the string through the peg's hole, and then lay the kinked end flat against the peg. Let the string run over it a couple of times as you turn the peg. *Tip:* Do not wind the plain (non-wound) part of a wound string around itself.

Long string

If a string happens to be way too long, you can first let it wind inwards for a few turns before guiding it back the other way. The last few turns must be wound directly onto the wood of the peg, and not over another part of the string. *Tip:* Four or five windings should be enough to prevent a string from slipping.

Leave space between windings and cheeks.

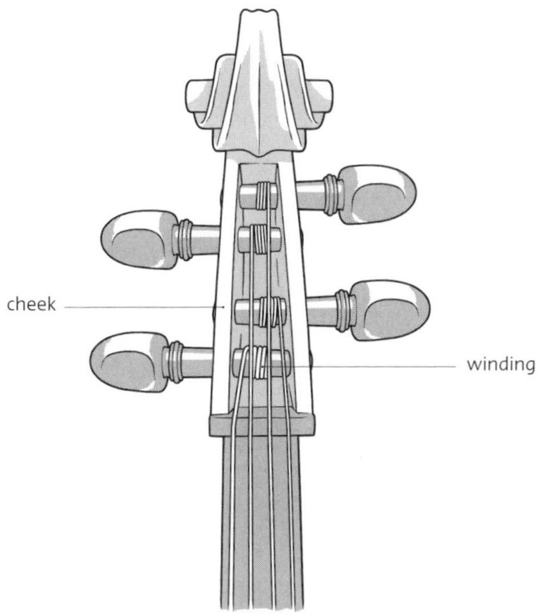

Space

Strings can break if they are jammed against the pegbox cheeks. So always make sure they have some space — unless you're in trouble because of a slipping peg (see page 139).

String sleeves

If you use string sleeves (see pages 73–74), slide them into place when the strings are nearly tuned. A sleeve does the most good on the E-string. Instead of a regular sleeve, many violinists use a tiny piece of vellum (parchment) under the string.

Protection

There are special fine tuners for gut strings. Other tuners may cut through the loop of a gut string in no time. You can extend the life of your strings with E-string protectors. Some violinists even use them for steel E-strings.

The loop of a gut string.

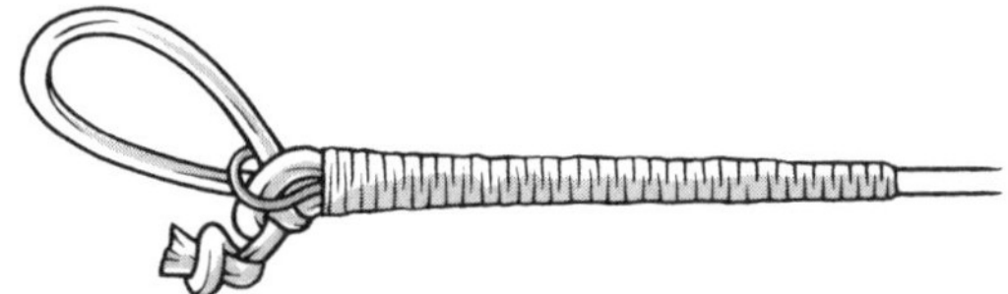

The first time

When you are replacing a string for the first time, you'll probably find you don't have enough hands. You need one to tighten, another to make sure the string doesn't come loose from the tailpiece, a third one to guide it through the grooves in the bridge and nut… So it's handy to have someone else around.

Grooves

When you replace your strings, check the pegs at the same time. Grooves in the pegs can damage your strings. If a peg won't 'grip' the string whatever you do, there's a chance that its hole is worn out.

Damage

Your strings can also be easily damaged by sharp edges on the bridge, the nut, or around the string-holes in the pegs. The grooves in the nut must be smooth and nicely rounded to prevent the strings from kinking. Check your instrument carefully if a string keeps breaking at the same point. If a string doesn't run smoothly across the nut or the bridge, rub a pencil point in the slots of the nut. This will leave some graphite dust that acts as a lubricant. If that doesn't do the trick, you'll need expert help.

Perfect fifths

On a properly tuned violin or viola, there is always a perfect fifth between one open string and the next (see page 118). You can check this by laying a pencil across two (perfectly tuned!) strings and pressing down so that they both touch the fingerboard. In both high and low positions, the difference in pitch between the two strings should always be a perfect fifth. If you have old strings, this may not be so, perhaps because one string is more stretched than the other. If so, the first will sound flat. Old strings are not the only possible cause if you don't hear perfect fifths; the bridge may be the culprit instead. Another tip: If you use traditional gut strings, you may not hear perfect fifths either.

THE BRIDGE

The bridge is held in place by the strings. Their tension also pulls the bridge forward and pushes it down. Altogether, the bridge has to withstand around sixty pounds of pressure — so do keep an eye on it.

Perpendicular

Now and then, you should check that the bridge hasn't started leaning forward, toward the fingerboard. If it does, you may carefully try to push it back in its original position yourself. Its back should be perpendicular to the violin's top. Don't hesitate to leave this to a violin maker or technician. Another check: Make sure that both feet are exactly lined up with the notches in the *f*-holes. If not, your instrument will not produce perfect fifths.

New bridge

If the downward pressure of the strings has made the bridge sag, you need a new one. The bridge also needs replacing:

- if the grooves have become too deep: No more than a third of the diameter of each string should be inside the groove;
- if you switch to different strings, the string height may need to be adjusted. This often requires a new or modified bridge;
- or if it's too flat (so that you accidentally play two strings instead of one), or too curved (making it difficult to play two or three strings at once).

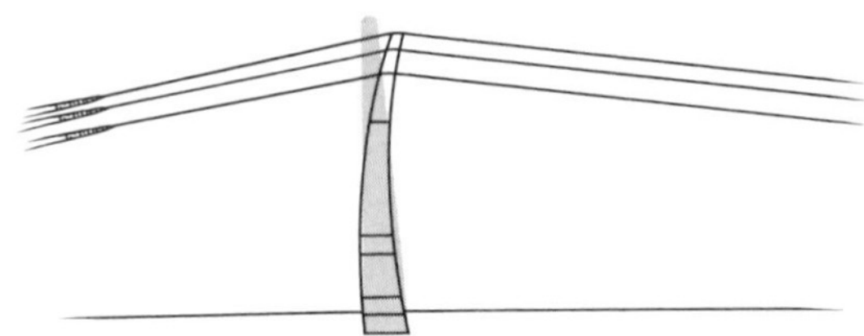

Bridge bending toward the fingerboard.

Summer and winter bridges

If you live in an area with marked seasonal changes, you may consider using two bridges: a higher one in the winter, as the lower humidity (see page 143–145) makes the wood shrink which reduces string height, and a lower one in the summer, when the reverse happens.

Custom-fit

A new bridge needs to be custom-fit to the violin, so that it has the right height and curve for the instrument, and so that its feet

A blank bridge and one made to fit the instrument (right).

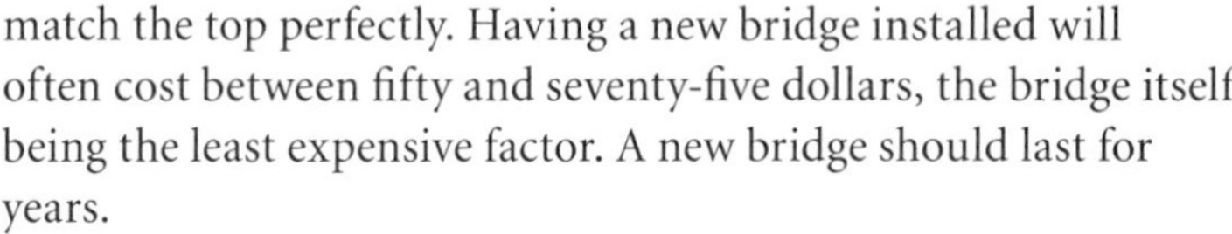

match the top perfectly. Having a new bridge installed will often cost between fifty and seventy-five dollars, the bridge itself being the least expensive factor. A new bridge should last for years.

More than carving alone

There are bridges with moveable feet which automatically adjust to the arch of the top — but even you prefer this type of bridge, it can't hurt to have a specialist install it. Again, properly fitting a bridge to an instrument involves more than carving the feet.

SOUND POST, LOOP, FINGERBOARD...

If you have bought a new violin, it's a good idea to have it checked after six months or a year. One example of what an expert might spot is that the sound post may have become slightly too short as a result of the wood not having settled completely when you bought the instrument.

The tailpiece loop

Another example would be that the tailpiece loop may have stretched. If so, the distance between tailpiece and bridge will now be too short, which may muffle the sound. The correct distance is between about 2.2" and 2.4" (5.5–6 cm) on a full-size violin, and about 2.75" on a viola. Adjustable tailpiece loops (also known as *tailpiece hangers* or *tail guts*) are available.

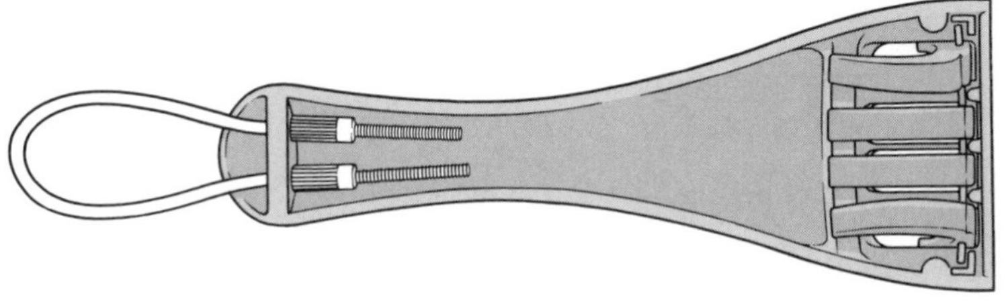

Tailpiece with an adjustable loop.

The fingerboard

However hard your fingerboard is, stopping the strings will wear grooves in it eventually, and your fingers will even create very shallow pits in the wood, especially if you perspire a lot. If you have a good, ebony fingerboard this is of course a very slow process. As an example, professional musicians, who play for many hours every day, often have their fingerboards reworked once a year or every two years. If your fingerboard has been reworked too often and has become too thin as a result, you can have a new one fitted for around a hundred and fifty to two hundred and fifty dollars and up.

Splinter

If a piece of wood breaks off — a splinter along the edge for instance — make sure to keep that area dry, and don't clean it. Take the instrument to a violin maker as soon as possible, and take the broken-off piece with you if you still have it. It's also best to see an expert if you find loose glue joints, or cracks. Do you feel like repairing these yourself? Don't!

Buzzes

A violin can start buzzing in all sorts of places. Some examples:

- The **nut or the saddle** may have come loose.
- If the bridge or the nut is **too low**, the strings may vibrate against the fingerboard.
- The **winding** of a string may be damaged.
- The **string ends** may vibrate if they are touching the pegbox or tailpiece.
- The **tailpiece** itself should not be touching the top or the chin rest at any point.
- While checking the tailpiece, have a look at the **fine tuners** too.
- Is the **chin rest** securely fastened?
- Are the **sleeves** around the strings in the right place?

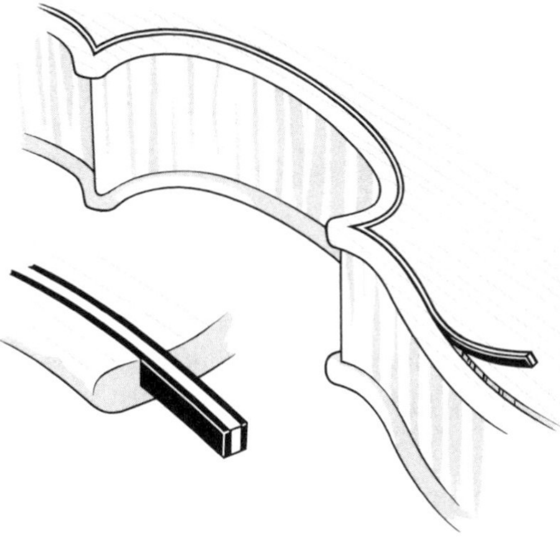

Purfling can work loose and cause buzzing.

- A **wire mute or loose purfling** can also cause noise, and so can an eye, or a decorative button on a tuning peg, or a loose glue joint.

DRY AIR

Wooden instruments are especially sensitive to dry air, and to rapid changes in humidity or temperature.

Freezing

Dry air is especially likely to be a problem if it is freezing outside and the central heating is on full blast. If humidity gets too low, the wood of your instrument will shrink. The result? If you're lucky, you'll only find that the string height is reduced, and that you need a winter bridge (see page 140). If you're not so lucky, the tuning pegs may come loose — and it may get even worse: The top, the back or any other parts may crack.

Hygrometer

The best level of humidity, both for bowed instruments and people, is often said to be around forty to sixty percent. A hygrometer is a device that allows you to keep an eye on the humidity level. You may have one in the room where you keep your violin, and some violin cases have one built-in. If the hygrometer shows that the air is getting too dry, it's time to do something about it.

Humidifiers

First, there are all kinds of small humidifiers that can be used inside the case, ranging from a very basic rubber tube with holes in it and a small sponge inside, to more complicated devices. Traditional humidifiers need a refill from time to time. Modern versions, which can both emit and absorb moisture, maintain the required relative humidity without refills. Two tips:

- If you move your instrument from a relatively humid environment to a much drier place, you may put a few **slices of potato** inside your case as a stop gap solution.
- Cases with a **built-in hygrometer** often feature a humidifier as well.

All-around solutions

If the humidity level is very low in your house, both you and your instrument (as well as your wooden furniture and floors) may benefit from a central humidifier—if your heating system allows for one—or a portable one. Some examples of the latter are steam humidifiers (affordable, fast, but possibly noisy) and 'cold' humidifier systems which are quieter but more expensive, take longer to work, and may need more frequent maintenance.

Some time to adjust

Always give your instrument some time to adjust to changes in temperature and humidity. For example, if it's freezing cold

Heaters and vents

Some don'ts: Never store a violin in direct sunlight, or near heaters, fireplaces, air-conditioning vents, or anywhere else where it may get too hot, too dry, or too cold — not even if it's in its case.

outside and you enter a warm room, leave your instrument in its case for fifteen minutes, or as long as you can. The more gradually things change, the better your instrument will like it.

ON THE ROAD

A few tips for when you travel with your violin:

- Make sure you have a **good case**, and check now and again to make sure that the handles and carrying straps are properly secured.
- In the car, your violin is safest **between the back and front seats**. The temperature is likely to be better there than in the trunk, and the chance of damage if you have an accident is smaller too. The worst place is under the rear window, especially on a sunny day, in full view of anyone who might fancy a violin.
- When you're in the train, tram, subway, or bus, keep your violin **on your lap**. It's safe, and you won't forget your instrument this way.
- Flying? Carry your instrument as **hand luggage**.
- If you still leave your instrument behind somewhere, you're more likely to get it back if your **contact information** is listed inside your case.

Insurance

Consider insuring your instrument, especially if you're taking it on the road — which includes visiting your teacher. Musical instruments fall under the 'valuables' insurance category. A regular homeowner insurance policy will not cover all possible damage, whether it occurs at home, on the road, in the studio, or onstage.

Tips

Companies that offer special insurances for musical instruments can be found in string players' magazines or online (see pages 214–

215). They may require you to have your instrument appraised before insuring it. Besides stating the value of the instrument, the appraisal report will also list various identifying features. You can list some of the essential data of your instrument yourself on pages 218–219. Two final tips:

- Most insurances do not cover **climatic factures.**
- Always check your insurance policy on the **conditions for air travel**.

12

History

You could write hundreds of pages about the violin and its centuries-old history, and there are plenty of writers who have done just that. That's why the history chapter in this book has been kept nice and short.

People have written so much about the history of the violin because it's a fascinating story as well as a very long one, and also because there is a lot of disagreement about many of its facets. A few things are known for sure, though.

Bow and arrow

In the days when supper was still something you hunted, our ancestors discovered that shooting an arrow produces a tone, due to the vibration of the bow's string. Many years later, someone found a way to amplify the feeble sound of the string by attaching a gourd to the bow. The soundbox was born.

A six-string, fretted viola da gamba.

The eighth century

The fact that you can also make a string vibrate by bowing it was only discovered much later. Exactly when is not certain, but bowed instruments were probably being played in ancient Persia, among other countries, as early as in the eighth century, and in Europe some time in the ninth century.

Fiddles

Apart from being used as a generic term for all bowed instruments, the word *fiddle* often refers to the instruments from the Middle Ages — and there were quite a few.

Lira da braccio

One of the best-known fiddles is the *lira da braccio*. Liras often had five or more strings, plus another two *bourdon strings* or *off-board drones*. These strings are not bowed or plucked, but they vibrate sympathetically with everything you play. The lira was played resting on the upper arm. '*Braccio*' is Italian for arm.

German viola

The lira da braccio is considered one of the predecessors of the violin and the viola. Originally, these instruments were played 'on the arm' as well, rather than held under the chin. Incidentally, the German word for viola, *Bratsche*, is derived from the Italian braccio.

Viola da gamba

Around the end of the fifteenth century, the first *viols* or *violas da gamba* were built. Contrary to the instruments da braccio, viols were played with the neck in an upright position. The smaller sizes were held with their tail on the knee of the musician; the larger ones were held between the legs ('gamba' is Italian for leg), like a cello.

The difference

Gambas are not just held differently. They also have sloped shoulders (like a double bass) and more strings, and they have frets, just like guitars do. These ridges across the neck make it easier to play the instrument in tune. On a fretted instrument, it is the exact position of the fret that produces the exact pitch, rather than the exact position of your finger. On a gamba, the frets are gut strings that are wound around the neck. Gambas are tuned differently as well.

Amateurs and professionals

Another difference is that gambas or viols, with their delicate, soft sound, were mainly played by wealthy amateur musicians. Braccios or violins, by contrast, were especially popular with folk and dance musicians, who often earned their living by playing. With a violin on your arm you can dance and walk around as you play, and a violin produces more volume than a gamba, which is always useful at noisy parties. Around two hundred years ago, the gamba gradually disappeared from the scene.

The cello and the double bass

The cello is in fact a member of the braccio family. Because of its size it's still played with its neck upright, the instrument standing between the legs of the musician. The double bass is a relative of both braccios and gambas. There's more about both instruments in the next chapter.

Amati and Stradivarius

The first violins were built in the first half of the sixteenth century. One of those early violins, built by Andrea Amati, has even survived. Stradivarius made the violin's arch a little less pronounced around 1700, resulting in a stronger sound. This didn't gain him immediate popularity. People were still used to the softer sound of violins with a higher arching. But in the years that followed, the demand for louder violins grew, especially because music was being performed in ever bigger halls.

From straight to curved

In that same period, the bow changed too. Curving the stick, which was originally straight, helped increase the volume potential of the instrument.

From gut to synthetic

The very first violins had non-wound gut strings. As early as the seventeenth century, it was discovered that the strings themselves could stay thinner if they were wound; the increased flexibility of thin, wound strings made them easier to play. The steel E-string became popular in the early 1900s, and the other steel strings followed some twenty years later. Synthetic-core strings came along in the 1950s.

13

The Family

The cello and the double bass are the two best-known relatives of the violin, but they're not the only ones. The following chapter is an introduction to the family of bowed instrument. The youngest relative — the electric violin — is covered in Chapter 9.

Violins and violas belong to the family of string or stringed instruments. They're also indicated as bowed instruments, which distinguishes them from plucked string instruments, such as guitars, banjos, and mandolins.

The cello

First the cello, which is not very different from the violin or the viola. The main difference is that it's quite a lot bigger. The four strings of the cello are tuned to the same notes as viola strings, only an octave lower (C2, G2, D3, A3). The instrument is often referred to using its original Italian name, violoncello. This literally means 'small, large violin.' Around 1700, Stradivarius built a cello which is still used as the standard model.

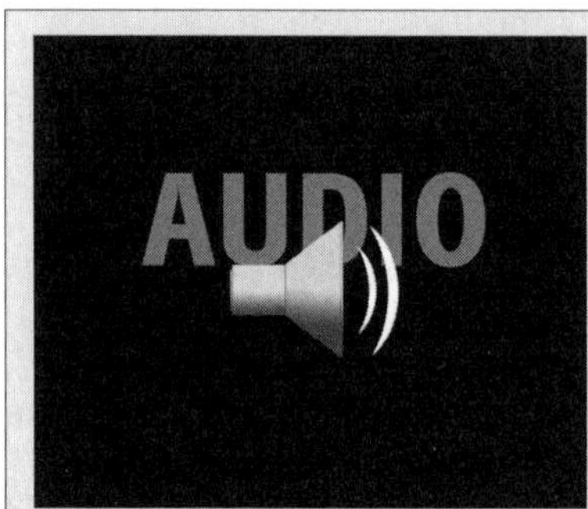

Tipcode VIOLIN-017
Tipcode Violin-017 provides brief demonstrations of a cello and of a plucked and bowed double bass.

Double bass

The double bass looks like an even bigger violin, but actually there are quite a few differences. It is not so much a big brother as a distant cousin. Unlike the violin or the cello, the bass usually has sloped shoulders, and the back is often flat — though there are swelled-back versions too. The tuning is different as well, the strings being a fourth apart, rather than a fifth. They're tuned to E, A, D, G, from low to high, similar to a bass guitar. Another difference is that a double bass has tuning machines, rather than wooden tuning pegs. The double bass is often used outside classical music, in which case it is usually plucked instead of bowed — again, like a bass guitar.

Bourdon strings

Most of the other relatives are rare. The old viola d'amore, for instance, is a kind of gamba with bourdon strings (see page 149) that is played like a violin. The Norwegian Hardanger fele is a smaller type of violin with four bourdon strings.

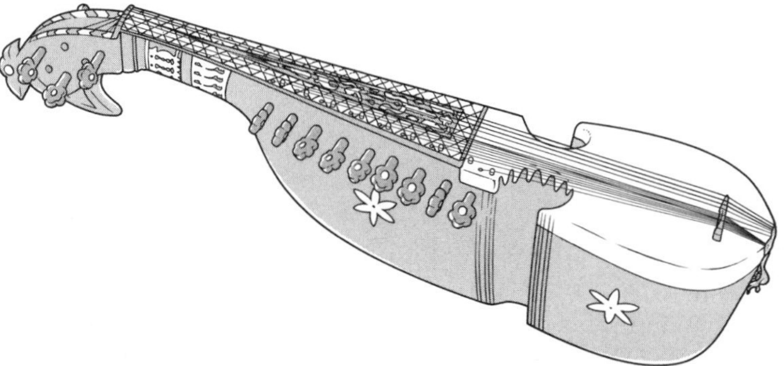

An Afghan rabab with twelve bourdon strings.

Rabab

There are many other bowed instruments with bourdon strings. The Afghan rabab or rebab shown below has twelve of them — but you may also come across rababs that have just two regular strings, and no bourdon strings at all. Just like other names, such as fiddle, the name rabab is used for a variety of bowed instruments.

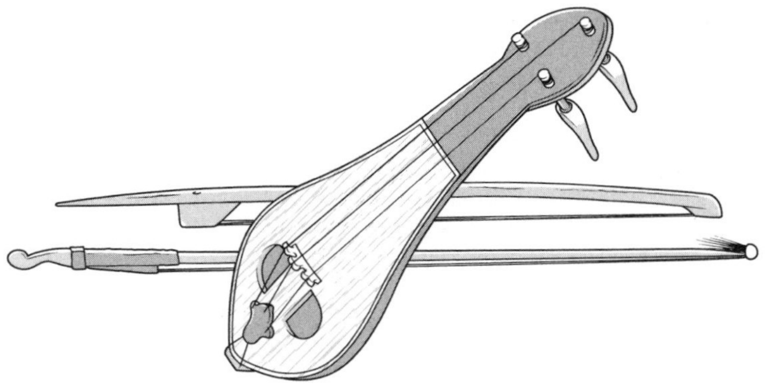

Classical kemenche.

Pear-shaped or elongated

The same goes for the kemenche. This refers to a small, pear-shaped instrument with three strings used in Turkish classical

music. But it can also indicate an elongated three-stringed instrument used to play folk music around the Black Sea and in Greece. The spelling varies as much as the shape, from kemânje to kamaché, and similar instruments are referred to as rababs or rebabs as well.
These instruments are usually mostly played with their tail on the knee of the musician, with the neck held upright. You may even see musicians who play a regular violin that way. And rebecs? They come with two, three, or more strings, with various body shapes, with or without frets...

With a fingernail

With some of these instruments, the different pitches are made not by stopping the strings on the fingerboard, but by touching them very lightly with a fingernail. The bow stick is often straight, and you tension the bow hair not with a frog but simply by wedging your fingers or your thumb between the stick and the hair.

Many more

Many other cultures have their own bowed instruments too, from the Japanese three- or four-string kokyu, the Chinese erhu, huqin, banhu, and sihu, to tubular Native American instruments.

Ergonomic instruments

A violin is not the most comfortable instrument to hold and play. As a result, violinists and violists often develop problems with their necks, arms, or fingers. To help prevent such symptoms,

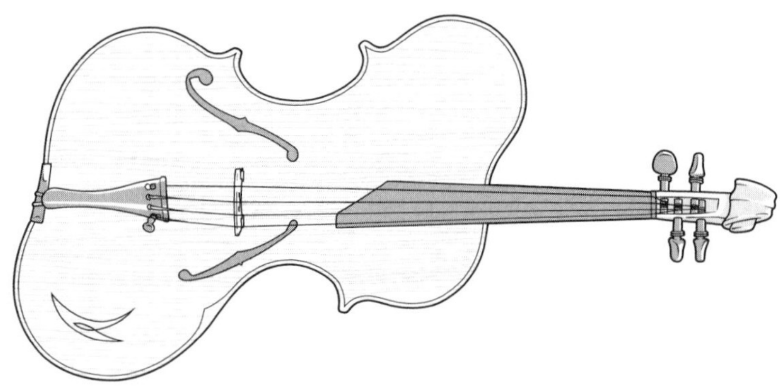

An ergonomic violin: the Pellegrina (David Rivinus)

some luthiers have designed ergonomic bowed instruments, such as the Pellegrina shown here.

14

How They're Made

Violins are still made in much the same way as they were hundreds of years ago, with chisels and files, with saws and planes, and with hide glue. Making a violin top the traditional way easily takes a couple of days' work.

In a violin factory, machines are used for parts of the process, such as roughly shaping all the wooden components. Master violin makers who build an instrument by themselves from start to finish, still do everything by hand. Somewhere in between these two extremes are the workshops that buy unvarnished *white violins*, which are finished by hand and then provided with fittings and strings.

Quarter-sawn wood is stronger that slab-cut wood.

Cake

The top and back are usually made of *quarter-sawn* or *quartered* wood — wood that has been sawed from the tree trunk in the shape of slices of cake. Each slice is then sawed almost in half to enhance the drying and seasoning process of the wood, which will make it less likely to warp, split, or shrink later on.

Bookmatched

This slice is later sawed through completely to create two separate halves. These halves are folded open, like a book, and then glued together. The result is the beginning of a *bookmatched plate*, the two halves being each other's mirror images. Not all plates are bookmatched.

Folded open like a book, then glued together.

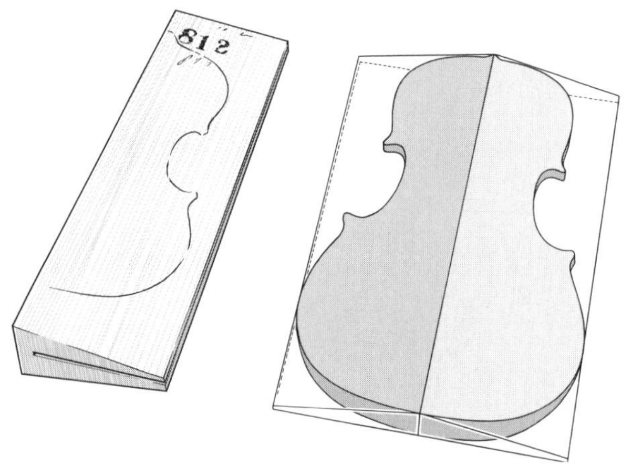

Carved

Traditionally, the top and the back are then carved into shape. Using dies and thickness gauges (graduation calipers), and simply by feel, the violin maker continuously checks to see if any more wood needs to be removed. The exact graduation is essential for the performance of the instrument.

The ribs

The ribs of the instrument are moistened so they can be shaped, and glued to the top, bottom, and corner blocks that strengthen them at the joints. The rib structure is assembled around a mold, which is of course later removed. The willow or spruce lining adds strength to the instrument, and the same strips of wood are necessary to glue the plates to the ribs.

Cut by hand

The *f*-holes and the channel for the purfling are traditionally cut by hand. Making the bass bar also takes a long time, as it has to be made to fit the inside arch of the top exactly.

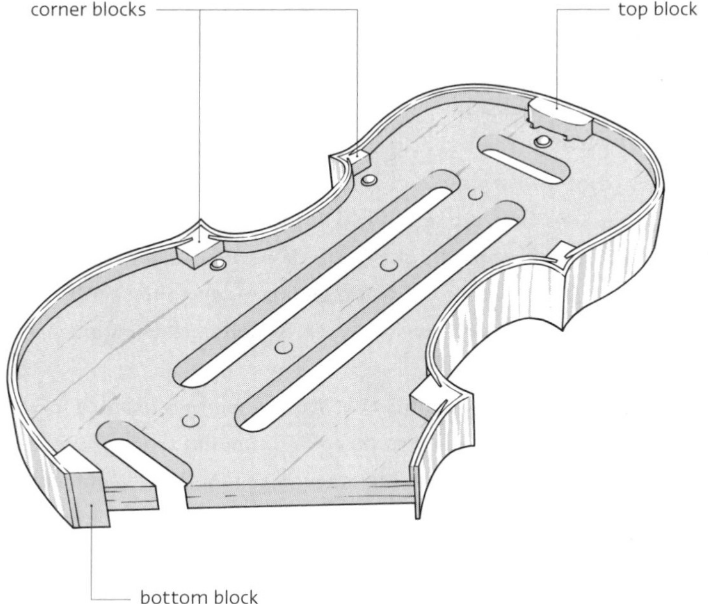

... assembled around a mold...

Jigsaw puzzle

The neck and scroll are carved from a single block of wood. The neck slots into the top block like a piece in a jigsaw puzzle. The weight of the fingerboard, which is made of heavy ebony, is reduced by hollowing out the underside.

From a single block...

Jigsaw puzzle...

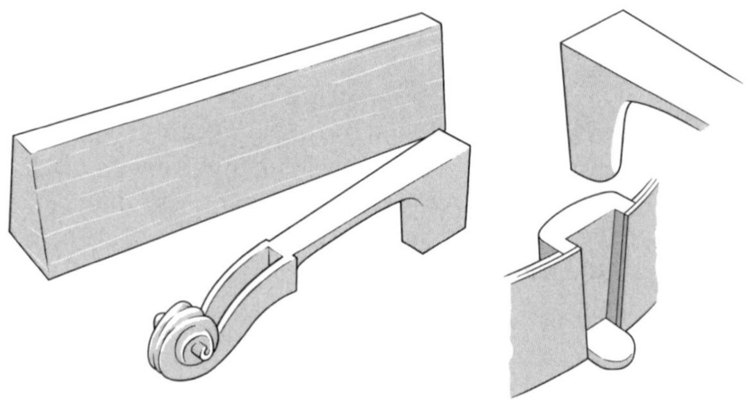

Wonderful stories

There are lots of wonderful stories told about the secret of those expensive old Italian violins. For instance, it is said that the wood used to make them was transported by dragging it behind a sailing ship, and that it is the salt sea water that gives the violins their special sound. Others say that the wood comes from centuries-old church towers which burned down; the wood was first broken in by vibrations from the church bells and then ripened by the fire... Or perhaps the varnish is the greatest 'secret' of those old violins — and the secret is safe, because the materials that were used back then are no longer available today.

A more recent theory claims that Italian winters used to last longer and summers used to be colder, making trees grow slower and thus produce a higher quality wood. The coldest era lasted from about 1645 to 1715, and Stradivarius built his best instruments between 1720 and 1720.

Mirror-smooth

Before it can be varnished, the wood has to be made mirror-smooth with a scraper. It is finished with a ground coat and then several coats of varnish. Violin makers often make their own varnish, so they can give their instruments exactly the shade they want.

Bows

The bow stick is first cut by hand and shaped over a flame. The horsehair is held in place in the frog and head by small wooden wedges.

15

Violin Brands and Makers

When you go out to buy a violin or a viola, you'll come across dozens of brand names — names of violin makers young, old, or dead, names of violin makers who never even lived, brand names and names of towns, and regions. This chapter sheds some light on the violin and viola market, and it introduces you to some of the old masters.

The majority of beginner's and student violins are made in China. Many of them bear Chinese names; others get German or Italian fantasy names, for example, and many American and international companies use their own brand names for Asian-made instruments.

Brand names

Some examples of familiar violin brand names would be **Becker**, **Otto Brückner**, **F. Cervini**, **Cremona**, **Glaesel**, **Knilling**, **Mathias Thoma**, **Meisel**, **Palatino**, **Scherl & Roth**, and **Wm. Lewis & Son,** and other names which are mentioned elsewhere in this chapter. Do note that this chapter is not intended to be complete, and that brand names may have been discontinued, sold, or changed by the time you read this.

Intermediate

Chinese luthiers make more expensive instruments as well, but there's more competition in those higher price ranges, for instance from older German or French instruments.

Germany

For many years, Germany was the main supplier of violins and violas in all price ranges, from beginner's instruments to master violins. Most affordable instruments are now made in Bubenreuth, by companies such as **Paesold**.

In Europe, these instruments sell for four to five hundred euros, including a case and a bow. To cut costs, many German-made violins use Chinese parts.

Workshop violins

Many German luthier families originally come from the area of Markneukirchen, Klingenthal, Adorf, and Schönbach (now named Luby). Workshop violins made in the first decades of the twentieth century fetch prices of some thousand to fifteen hundred euros — but there are more expensive instruments available as well.

Mittenwald

The German town of Mittenwald houses a famous Violin Making School, which was founded in 1858. Many luthiers choose Mittenwald as their residence.

Czech Republic and Rumania

In the Czech Republic, the city of Luby (formerly known as Schönbach) is the national centre of violin making. Rumania has a long violin making history as well. Most luthiers can be found in the city of Rhegin.

France

France has been a main player on the violin market for a long time. Some two hundred years ago, the small town of Mirecourt — the French center of violin making — housed the world's first violin factory, which employed some six hundred people. In Europe, French instruments from the early twentieth century tend to fetch slightly higher prices than otherwise similar German instruments, with a price range from thirteen hundred to two thousand euros.

German or French

Some find the sound of French workshop violins to be a bit richer or more complex, compared to German instruments — but there are others who think that French violins sound brighter, or louder. Most importantly, just listen to the instruments you're playing and don't bother where they're from. When choosing an instrument, the main thing that counts is how it sounds.

Other countries

In most countries you'll be able to find master violin makers who make high-quality instruments entirely by hand, usually to order. Most of them also sell used instruments, bows, and accessories, and they repair and rebuild instruments too.

(Master) violin makers

Not everybody who uses the name 'violin maker' is a master violin maker. Some mainly do repairs of student and intermediate violins, or they specialize in expensive instruments only; others concentrate on finishing and setting up white violins (see page 160), and so on. The exact number of master violin makers is unknown, but there must be over a hundred of them in the US alone. Most countries have an association or federation of violin and bow makers, which you'll be able to trace online or in string players' magazines (see page 214).

OLD MASTERS

Many books list the stories of dozens or even hundreds of violin makers from the past, where and when they lived and worked, and what their instruments could be worth today. Here's a very brief introduction to some of the most famous names in violin making.

Italy

The most famous Italian violins were built in the town of Cremona, from the sixteenth century onwards. **Andrea Amati** (1525-1611) was one of the first violin makers. His grandson **Nicolo Amati** taught the craft to **Francesco Ruggieri** (1620-c.1695), the most famous member of another important Cremonese violin-making family.

Stradivarius

Another of Nicolo's pupils was **Antonio Stradivari** (often referred to as Stradivarius), who lived from 1644 to 1737. Apart from violins and cellos, Stradivarius also made harps and guitars. Of his bowed instruments, around six hundred have survived. **Carlo Bergonzi** and **Joseph Guarnerius del Gesu** (1698–1744), the best-known member of the Guarnerius family, were among Stradivarius' apprentices.

Outside Cremona

Apart from the Cremonese school or style, to which all of these violin makers belonged, there were also Venetian, Milanese, and other schools. Each school of makers had its own characteristics, such as the shape of the f-holes and the exact model of the body. Experts can often tell a master violin's maker by simply looking at the scroll.

Brescian school

Double purfling, a characteristic of the Brescian school is rare, but you may come across it. One of the best known representatives of the Brescian school, **Gasparo di Bertolotti** a.k.a. **Gasparo da Salò**, is often said to have made the first viola.

Germany

Jacob Stainer, who died in 1683, is often seen as the founder of German violin making. Until well into the eighteenth century, a violin made by Stainer was more expensive than a Stradivarius; the latter was often considered 'too loud.' **Mathias Klotz I** (1656–1743), who was very important for violin making in Mittenwald, studied under Stainer and Nicolo Amati. Instruments made by the slightly younger **Sebastian Klotz** are still highly prized. One of the major violin-making families in the German town of Klingenthal was the **Hopf** family, including Caspar (1650–1711) and his grandson David.

France

Two important French violin masters were **Nicolas Lupot** (1758–1824) and, from Mirecourt, **Jean Baptiste Vuillaume** (1798–1875).

England

The best-known English violin name is **Hill**. Hill's bows are still famous, and you often find the description 'Hill model' on tailpieces, tuning pegs, and other parts.

The Netherlands

Violins made by the Dutch luthiers **Hendrik Jacobs** (1630–1704) and **Johannes Cuypers** (1766–1828) are usually valued at about twenty-five to fifty thousand dollars.

16

Tips on Practicing

Practicing doesn't seem to be every musician's favorite pastime, and that goes for musicians at all levels and ages. Why? Because most musicians want to play their favorite music, rather than spending hours playing scales, etudes, or arpeggios. Because, oftentimes, progress doesn't show right away. And because learning to play an instrument is about long-term gratification, and we seem to have lost touch with that concept. Or because... A number of reasons. But still, it needs to be done — and it can be entertaining, too!

This chapter offers helpful hints on how to practice efficiently, turning practice sessions into rewarding and even inspiring events. Ineffective practice habits are as much work as effective ones, but yield no progress and may cause you to quit playing entirely. Also included in this chapter are helpful tips on where and when to practice, the various components of a good practice session and how to structure it, practice techniques, the importance of memorizing music, and much more.

Sports

Practicing is to music what training is to sports, but there are some major differences. Firstly, most sportsmen train with their teammates, while practicing is something you usually do alone. Secondly, if you play football, soccer, or any other type of sport, you'll probably have a match every week.

Most musicians don't have that many opportunities to perform — and usually, being able to perform is why you practice in the first place.

Joining a band

That's why it's important to play in a band, an ensemble, or an orchestra: This offers performance opportunities, it's a great way to meet new friends, and it provides you with clear and realistic goals. Practicing so you can play your part at the next rehearsal is a better motivation than practicing because, well, you're supposed to.

One note

Joining an ensemble is even more important if your play violin, cello, flute, saxophone, or any of the other instruments that typically produce one note at a time. These instruments are best suited for group settings, or should at least be accompanied by a piano, for example.

Chords

The piano, keyboards, and guitars are better suited to playing just by yourself, without a band or another form of accompaniment — but even then, playing with other musicians is both fun and inspiring.

Keep on going

It's clear that practice is necessary to achieve a certain level. But should you continue to practice once you've reached a level you're happy with? Maybe not — but if this means that you're limited to playing the same pieces over and over, boredom may set in and the end of your musical endeavors may be near.

No practicing

So can you play without practicing? Of course you can. There are thousands of garage band musicians who never practice; they just play with their friends, and they're having a ball doing so. However, they will usually stop playing once they get a little older, and having no real musical basis, it's unlikely that they'll pick up an instrument again later on in life.

Recreational music making

Participating in a drum circle, for example, allows anyone to play music with a group of people without any prior experience. These and other recreational music-making activities are about socializing, reducing stress, and relaxation more than striving for musical prowess. (Incidentally, that's what most garage bands are about, too.)

Means, goal, or making music?

Some tend to see practice as a goal in and of itself; and the goal is achieved by practicing, say, a half an hour a day. Others consider practice a means to an end — the end usually being the ability to play well (at whatever level) and to perform successfully. You can also consider practice as making music, as a journey that leads

Not another obligation

If you want to pursue a career in music, your practice habits should foster diligence, hard work, and making sacrifices (though the latter may not be considered as such). If you don't, practicing should probably be more about fun than about obligations.

to who knows where, and the journey itself is what it's all about. Teachers who make you understand and feel why playing scales is so essential, help you enjoy this journey.

How long — or how?

One of the most frequently asked questions is, 'How long should I practice?' You could certainly structure your practice sessions to last a required number of minutes per day. But wouldn't it be more interesting to look at what should or could be achieved, so your focus would be on accomplishing a particular task, rather than on filling time? Still, no matter how you look at it, you do need to invest some time in practice, and it's essential to be able to gauge how much time that typically is; so that's what the next section addresses.

The youngest musicians

For very young musicians, things are a bit different. Most experts seem to agree that you can't really speak of 'practicing' until kids are some five or six years of age. For these kids, it's more about spending quality time and having fun with their instrument (if they've actually already chosen one) than about trying to achieve something other than a long-lasting love for music. Playing up to five or ten minutes a day will be fine. The shorter these sessions last and the more fun they are, the more likely a child will want to play three, four, or more days per week.

Six and up

As children get a little older, they'll be able to focus for longer periods, and they'll start to grasp the concept of doing things now that will pay off later. They will also be ready to maintain a practice routine with their teacher's and your guidance. Six- to eight-year-olds should typically spend some fifteen minutes per day on an instrument, say four to six days per week. The older they get, the longer they will be able, and willing, to play.

Half an hour

If you're older — twelve and up — most teachers will probably tell you that playing half an hour a day will help you make sufficient progress to keep things interesting. If you practice effectively, however, you may be able to do your assignments in less time. (This can be so rewarding that you end up playing longer than you intended!)

Short and often

For kids, a practice session lasting a half an hour can be quite long, though, and it may be better to divide the routine up into three ten-minute sessions, or even six sessions of five minutes each. You can do so yourself, too: Short sessions tend to be more effective, with improved retention and more focus.

Much longer

The better you get, the more you need to practice to progress and maintain your abilities at a desired level. Music majors often practice three to five hours a day. The longer you practice, the sooner you will find that not practicing decreases your musical abilities — so you have to keep up all, or most, of the time!

Music, not minutes

Rather than focusing on a certain amount of time you need to practice, you can look at what should or could be achieved by practicing so you can focus on a set goal (and the music) rather than at the minutes passing by. In order to do so, you must understand exactly what your teacher expects (or you need to be able to set your own goals), and you need to be able to self-assess whether you've achieved those goals.

Assignments

For teachers, this means that they need to be very explicit about their assignments. For example, rather than simply telling you to 'learn to play that piece,' they must state specific criteria, (i.e., 'play it with the metronome at 148 beats per minute,' or 'play a scale five times, without any mistakes, at a certain minimum tempo'). This way, you can simply tell when you've completed the assignment. If the teacher also conveys the practice techniques you need to most effectively reach the goals set for that week, practicing will be much more than a thirty-minute routine to be endured. It also puts things into your own hands, rather than in the clock's hands...

Your own teacher

Practicing is something that needs to be learned (and often taught). When you practice alone, you're expected to catch your own mistakes, to discover what prompted them, to fix them, and to find a way to prevent them in the future. In effect, when you practice, you are your own teacher. That's not an easy thing to be.

At home

And after all that, when you get to your next lesson or performance, you may find that you're not able to play what you could play at home. Or could you? Did you really hear everything that went wrong? Did you repeat everything to a point where you could even play it under pressure? Probably not — and playing in front of a teacher, your family, or any other type of audience is quite different from playing when there's no one around. This can be practiced too, though. Simply ask your roommate, your kids, friends, or anyone else to come listen to the new piece you have — hopefully — mastered. Getting experienced in playing for others is an important part of the learning process.

When

Ideally, practicing becomes a daily routine; something which is as natural as having dinner, or brushing your teeth. And just like most people have dinner or brush their teeth around the same time every day, practicing is more likely to become a natural part of the day when you do it at or around a set time. Spending time with your instrument on a regular basis may be more important than how much practice you actually do, initially.

Every day?

Should you practice every day? It's unlikely that anything you *have* to do seven days a week will be a lot of fun. That's why many experts will advise you that practicing five to six days will do to make sufficient progress.

Which day?

Sunday often sounds like a good day to skip practicing — but it's also the day of the week that allows for more time to practice, and practicing on Sundays still leaves plenty of time for other activities.

A closer look

If you're having lessons, the day before your lesson is usually the worst one to skip. Also note that it's often very effective to have a short practice session right after your lesson or later that same day. This reinforces the lesson content, and it's a perfect opportunity to take a close look at your weekly assignments.

No time

If it's simply to busy for your intended practice routine, try to sit down and just play one of your favorite pieces, or something else you like to play, rather than not playing at all. Keeping in touch with your instrument is really important.

When?

For many people, it seems best to practice at a set time (such as before school, right after work, before or after dinner). Others prefer to schedule their practice time around other obligations. That way, they can play when they feel like it, rather than having to do so because it happens to be 6:00 PM. Here are some additional tips on planning practice sessions:

- **For students**: Practicing before doing homework provides a nice break between your academic activities, but it may be hard to focus on music if you have lots of homework to do.
- Waiting until **after homework** to practice may feel as if you're never finished; it's like one obligation after the other.
- Planning a practice session **before your favorite TV show** (which is then the reward for practicing) may be more successful than trying to get up and practice when the show is over.

Holidays

It's really important that you keep to your practice sessions during (school) holidays as well. If you don't touch your instrument for a couple of weeks, the first lessons and practice sessions after the holiday may be quite frustrating as you probably won't be able to play those same pieces anymore. You may consider a holiday practice schedule, though.

How?

People all have their own ways of handling assignments, most likely approaching them the same way they do other things in life. Teachers can help you apply your personal way of handling things to your practice sessions, making them as efficient as possible. Some examples:

- If you're not good at **focusing your attention**, don't start three new pieces at once.
- If you're **afraid to start new pieces**, you may tend to keep on 'practicing' songs you already play very well — so you're dedicating time to practicing, but you're not likely to make any progress.
- If you're **not aware of the mistakes** you make, you will end up rehearsing those mistakes, and it'll be hard to reverse and 'deprogram' those errors. The solution is to learn how to evaluate your own playing before moving on.

Record your music

No matter how good you are, it's always hard to judge you own playing as you play. Tip: record your practice session, or your first or subsequent attempts to play the piece that you have been practicing, and then judge your performance by listening to the recording, once or a couple of times. This is very instructive for musicians at any level. Also consider recording your lessons, so you can listen once more to what was said, and especially how you sounded, when you get home. All you need is a portable recording device with a built-in microphone — although better equipment yields better and more enjoyable results.

WHERE

Ideally, you should be able to practice whenever you feel like it, without being hindered and without hindering others. A practice space needn't be large, just enough to accommodate you and your instrument. If there's room for the instrument to remain unpacked between practice sessions, no valuable time (or inspiration!) gets lost by having to unpack and assemble it before each practice. Ideally, again, you should be able to grab your instrument, tune it if necessary, and play. There are various types of floor-standing and wall-mounted stands on which string, wind, and other small instruments can sit unpacked and out of the way of people, pets and other damaging circumstances. Special covers are also available to help protect your valuable investments against dust and airborne dirt.

Music stand

If you read sheet music, you will need a music stand. This affordable piece of hardware promotes good posture (and prevents sore necks), provided it has been set up at the correct height. Nearly all music stands can be folded into a compact size, but it's easier if they can be left standing for the next practice session. This also enhances their life expectancy, as they may be quite flimsy. Do you need to bring a stand to lessons or recitals? Then invest in a second stand to be kept in the instrument case or bag, if possible, so you can't forget to bring it.

More on music stands

A basic music stand will set you back less than twenty dollars. Tip: Most music stands have two 'arms' that keep the sheet music in place and prevent music books from flopping closed. If yours doesn't, you can use a rubber band or clothes pins, or you can have your music books spiral-bound so that they stay open. One more tip: Music stands are also available in bright colors and heavy-duty versions.

Light

Lighting in the room should be sufficient to see the music easily and clearly. An additional small lamp is usually all that takes. Tip: There are special lamps available for music stands specifically.

Stool or chair

A regular stool or chair will usually do. Pianists, keyboard players, drummers, and other musicians are better off using a special (preferably height-adjustable) stool or bench. Without it, posture may be bad and practicing can be tiresome.

Metronome

A metronome is a small mechanical or electronic device that ticks or bleeps out a steady adjustable pulse, so you can tell immediately if you're dragging or speeding. This way, a metronome can help you develop your inner clock.

Slow

It's also a great device to use when practicing entire pieces or difficult bits very slowly, and it can help you improve your speed on the instrument step by step. Like any other tool, metronomes should be used wisely. Using one isn't a very good idea with a

Two mechanical metronomes and two electronic ones.

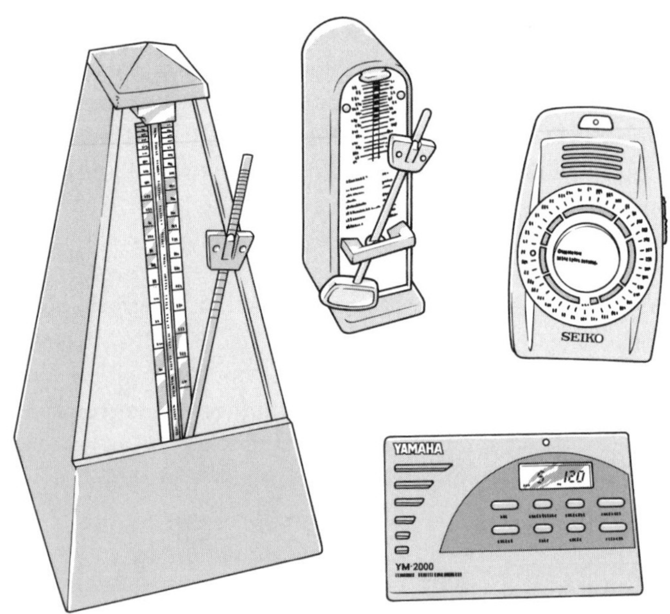

new piece, or when you're focusing on your tone, for example. Also, if you use it too often, you may become dependent on it. Metronomes are available starting at less than twenty dollars.

Tuning devices

Most electronic metronomes can also sound a 440 Hz tuning tone (the standard A to which most instruments are tuned; see page 115). For more information about tuning devices, please check out Chapter 10.

Sound systems and computers

Putting up a sound system in your practice area allows you to play along to prerecorded music, play back a recorded lesson, or maybe even record the practice session. Likewise, a computer can be used to play back CDs, DVDs, and CD-ROMS; to access online lessons and music games; or to record practice sessions (if equipped with the right hardware and software). It's also a helpful tool to compose, arrange, transpose, or create music. Synthesizers, home keyboards, and other digital instruments can be hooked up directly to the computer using MIDI, the musical instrument digital interface that is part of all digital music equipment.

And more

There's much more you can do to make practice more effective and fun. Here are some additional tips:

- Consider **lightening up** on practice arrangements if you're very busy. Play your instrument to relax rather then to study.
- Try playing in **another room** of the house from time to time, or even outside, if possible.
- Make sure your practice time is **uninterrupted**, and ask people who call to call back.
- **Varying the structure** of your practice sessions can help keep things fresh. Have your main focus on playing a new piece for a month or so, then address sound production or intonation for a couple of weeks, and so on.
- If you want to practice an hour or more per day, do take one or more **short breaks**. Very brief micro-breaks help you stay

focused. If you just can't get that one difficult passage down, comb your hair, pet the cat, eat a carrot, or take a sip of water before trying again. Or try again next week!

- Your instrument should be in **good repair** and tuned properly.
- **Stop if it hurts**. Playing an instrument should not induce pain. If the pain (back, fingers, neck, lips — anywhere) returns every time you practice or play, consult a teacher. The solution could be as simple as getting a different chair or resetting the music stand.

THE COMPONENTS

One of the main keys to effective practice is to have well-structured practice sessions. Depending on your level of playing, the main components of a practice session are:

- Warming up
- Scales and arpeggios
- Etudes
- Sight-reading
- New pieces
- Review

If you're a beginning student, the list will be shorter, and elements will be added as you progress.

Tuning

Most instruments need to be tuned, or the tuning needs to be checked, before you can play. This is where the practice session really begins. As said before, it is easiest if the instrument is always ready to be played — unpacked and assembled. You may want to have valuable and vulnerable instruments covered or packed when they're not being played, however. Also, parts such as strings, and

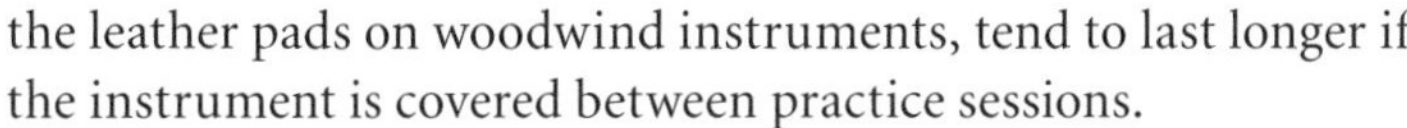

the leather pads on woodwind instruments, tend to last longer if the instrument is covered between practice sessions.

Warming up

Playing music requires a warm up, just like sports do: You may even get injured if you play demanding pieces without a decent warm up. For beginners and intermediate players, the few minutes of 'warming up' are basically meant to get into mood for playing, to get the fingers going, and to get 'into the instrument.' In that sense, it even helps if you take a good long look at your instrument before you play your first notes. Warm-up exercises are not technically demanding; they're the ideal setting for focusing on tone quality, because you can really listen to the sound you're producing.

Scales, arpeggios and etudes

Scales and arpeggios (broken chords) are often used for warm ups, but they're also practiced separately. They're technical exercises that increase your playing proficiency, so your fingers will be able to do what your mind tells them to. Etudes are pieces written with that same goal in mind.

More fun

Many musicians dislike playing scales, etudes, and similar exercise material; it's not as much fun as 'real' pieces, and such exercises often seem meaningless. A good teacher may be able to make you understand why they're so essential, inspiring you to play them with all your heart (though a little less will usually do). Besides, there are various ways to make playing scales and etudes more fun. Some ideas?

- **Focusing on your tone** really helps; imagine what a scale would sound like when played by your all-time favorite musician!
- Playing scales as if they were **beautiful pieces of music** makes a difference too.
- Make the **volume go up** as you play the scale upwards, and vice versa.

- **Speed up** when playing upwards, and vice versa.
- Speed up and **get louder** one way, and vice versa.
- Play scales in the rhythm of **a song you like**, or play them as triplets.
- Do you play the piano, too? Play F-major with **your left hand** and C-major with **your right hand**, and experiment with other pairs of scales.

New pieces

Adding new pieces is necessary to keep progressing, to keep yourself challenged, to expand your repertoire, and to raise your general level of playing. Check pages 188–190 for tips on handling new pieces.

Reviewing repertoire

When you play pieces you already know, there's no struggle, so you're simply playing music. It's as close to performing as practicing will get — and that's what playing is all about, for most musicians. Reviewing older pieces also keeps your repertoire alive.

Sight-reading

Sight-reading is as essential part of various exams and competitions: You're given a new and unfamiliar piece of music to read and play or sing on demand. It's much the same as reading a story or an article to someone, albeit that playing while reading music is quite a bit harder than reading text aloud. Sight-reading is an important skill for all musicians who want or need to play in situations where they will be expected to perform or rehearse without prior preparation.

And more

A practicing session can consist of lots of other components, such as:

- **Specific exercises** (dynamics, phrasing, improvisation, ear training, extending your range with higher or lower notes, etc.).
- **Experimenting**: Explore the instrument, try to discover new sounds or playing techniques, try to figure out a melody you've heard, think up new melodies...

- **Playing along** with prerecorded music or special play-along recordings. This is a valid, fun, and effective technique for any musician who doesn't have a band or an orchestra at their disposal. You can also record a performance or rehearsal of the band or orchestra you're in, and use that.

Recitals

Have you added a new piece to your repertoire and can you really play it? Again, try playing for friends or housemates. These brief, informal recitals can be very effective. They offer you an opportunity to perform, they may help diminish performance anxiety and they teach you to continue playing through mistakes — and you're most likely to make at least a few of those the first time you play a new piece.

TIP

Maintenance

Some instruments require a bit of maintenance at the end of each practice session. Wind instruments have to be disassembled and dried, orchestral string instruments will need the hair of their bows slackened, guitar and bass guitar strings need to be cleaned, and so on. Specific instructions can be found in the relevant chapter of this Tipbook.

STRUCTURE

To get the most out of your practice sessions, you need to structure them, planning ahead what it is you want to get done.

The beginning and the end

It's usually best to start with things that are relatively easy to play, such as scales. You may also prefer to start each session with a piece you already know. Starting off with an unfamiliar piece can be quite frustrating. Ending the session with a review of familiar repertoire is like a reward for having practiced.

The same order?

You may prefer the safety of doing things in the same order every time; others dislike such routine and rather vary the order of their practice components from day to day.

Two or three sessions

If you divide your practice time into two or more sessions, it's probably most effective to do a little of everything in each session rather then spending the first session only on scales, the second on a new piece, the third on older repertoire, etc. — but then you might just prefer that.

Clock?

Some experts advise you to dedicate a certain amount of time to each component: a five minute warm-up, ten minutes or etudes, ten on a new piece, and another five to play something familiar. Others will tell you to get rid of the clock, as you want to focus on what you're playing rather than on the minutes passing by.

Short, medium, long

The clearer your musical goals are, the easier it will be to practice effectively. When defining these goals, it often helps to distinguish:

- **long-term goals**: I'd like to join such-and-such band, or play a solo recital by the end of the year or this month...
- **mid-term goals**: I'd like to finish this method book, or be able to play these pieces...
- **and short-term goals**, which may differ for each practice session: I'd like to memorize this piece, or play that section ten times without a mistake...

PRACTICING TECHNIQUES

Practicing efficiently is also a matter of applying the right practicing techniques. Improving your tone requires a different technique than increasing your speed, or tackling a new piece.

Small jobs

One of the best ways to make your practice session more effective and fun is to break down large jobs into a number of small jobs. Rather than tackling a new piece from beginning to end, break it down into four or eight measures to be played per day, for example. This way, you can have a small success every day, rather than fighting to master the entire piece in one week.

Revision

If a new piece is broken up into sections comprised of a number of bars, reviewing the sections that were done on previous days should be an essential part of each practice session. Learning an instrument is most effectively done through frequent repetition. (In various languages, the word for 'practice' literally means repetition!)

The right notes

Repetition results in long-term memory storage, which is good. The problem, however, is that your memory does not select what should be stored and what should not. If you consistently repeat an incorrect passage, that's what will be stored, and if you play the wrong note half of the time, there's a fifty-fifty chance that the wrong note will come out at your performance. So when repeating things, make sure you play the right notes — and slow down as much as you need on order to do so.

Five or ten

Some teachers may advise you to move to the next section only when you're able to play the current section correctly five (or ten) times in a row. If you make a mistake, you start counting all over again — until you get all five (or ten) correct. Others may not be concerned with the number of repetitions, so long as you play it right the final time: This way, your fingers are supposed to 'remember' the right moves.

Slow down

A difficult passage may be hard to play correctly, and playing it right five times in a row may seem impossible. The solution, again, is to slow things down. Slow, in this case, means really slow. Take one, two, or more seconds for every note, and disregard note values for now. Take a metronome, set it at sixty BPM (i.e., sixty Beats Per Minute, equaling one beat per second), and let it tick one, two, or more times before moving on to the next note. Such slow tempos make you aware of the movements your fingers have to make to get from note to note, or from chord to chord.

Tone

For advanced players, practicing a piece really slowly is also a good way to work on their tone, and to get the smallest nuances of a piece right: dynamics, intonation, phrasing, and everything else beyond hitting the right notes at the right time.

A NEW PIECE

There are also various practicing techniques for handling new pieces. As mentioned before, a piece can be divided up into four bar, eight bar, or longer sections, revising the previous sections (and playing them absolutely correctly) before moving on. This is just one of many approaches, and all of these approaches can be mixed to come up with a combination that is most effective for you.

Challenge

Starting a new piece is a positive challenge to some, while it makes others feel as if they have to start all over again. Of course, avoiding new pieces will yield no progress. Also, learning to tackle new pieces can help you tackle other problems and deal with new, complex subjects as well — which is just one of the reasons that music students perform better in various academic fields. Some of the tips below apply to more advanced musicians only; others work for beginners too.

Listen

As said before, it is essential that you practice a piece playing only the correct notes. It helps if you can first listen to a recorded version of the new piece so you know what it's supposed to sound like before attempting to play it. Of course, you can also ask your teacher to play the piece for you.

Read along

Reading along while listening to a new piece helps you link the notes to the music. With complex pieces, study the part visually before listening to it, so you won't be surprised by repeats and other markings. Reading the music before playing it also gives you the opportunity to check out all dynamic signs and tempo markings, to locate accidentals (flats, sharps, naturals), and numerous other details and characteristics of the piece — and you don't have to worry about playing the instrument at the same time you're reading.

More

If you have a teacher, ask him or her to tell you about the new piece of music: its general character, its form (12-bar blues or 32-bar AABA? Rondo or suite?), the style, the composer, the era in which it was written, and so on. After all, there's more to music than simply executing the composer's notes.

Step by step

Beginning players are often advised to approach a new piece step by step. First, clap the rhythm of the notes, counting aloud as you go. When you've got the rhythm down, play the melody without paying attention to the rhythm. Once you can clap the rhythm and play the right notes, combine the two — very, very slowly. This approach works well for advanced players too. Pianists and other keyboard players can practice the left hand part first, and then the right hand, before attempting to play a new piece with both hands.

The trouble spots

Alternatively, depending on your ability and the complexity of the piece, you can play the piece through at an easy tempo, spotting the difficult bits as you go. Playing a piece as such, with mistakes and all, may give you a general idea of what it is about (assuming you haven't heard it before). Other players rather start by locating the tricky bits and figure them out first. A tip: If you're working on a tricky section, always include a few notes or bars before and after that particular section in order to make the tricky section a part of the whole thing, rather than an isolated hurdle that might scare you off every time you see it coming.

Analyzing the trouble spots

If you're having a problem with a certain section, you can simply play it again and again (and again) until you get it right. However, it might be more effective to find out what's causing the problem in the first place. Is it the fingering (which fingers to use for which note)? The rhythm? Or can you not play the part with your left hand while your right hand is doing something else? Or is it a note higher or lower than you can play or sing? Without proper answers to those questions, it will be hard to move on — and before you get to the answers, you need to come up with the right questions. Again, this is something a teacher may be able to help you with. One step beyond analyzing the trouble spots is developing exercises that help the student tackle them. This is something advanced players do for themselves, and something that teachers should teach their students.

MEMORIZING MUSIC

Opinions differ as to whether you should memorize music. Some teachers insist that you should; others feel that memorizing music should be optional, unless you're considering a professional career in music.

Why?

Why would you learn to memorize a piece that can simply read?

- It can help make you a **better musician**. If you don't have to focus on reading, you can fully focus on other elements — tone, phrasing, dynamics, and so on — and listen to yourself play. Also, to play from memory you have to really know a piece inside out, which can only help improve your performance.

- It makes you **look good**. Professional soloists play without sheet music, so why can't you?
- On some instruments, playing by heart allows you to **watch your hands** as you play. Not a very professional approach, but it can be handy.

Why not?

Of course, there's no need to keep musicians from memorizing music (and some are extremely good at it), but why force them?

- Being required to play without sheet music makes a performance an **even more stressful** event — and wasn't making music about enjoying yourself?
- Worrying about what'll happen if you **forget the piece** does not inspire a good performance. It takes away more energy from the music than reading notes does. In other words, some just need sheet music to play well, even while others might play better without it.
- If you're **not good at memorizing** music, learning pieces by heart may take up valuable time that's probably better spent on things you can do to grow musically. Do note that learning to memorize music takes time too: It's not something you just can do.

Techniques and tips

There are various ways and techniques to memorize music. What works great for you, may not work for your friend, and vice versa. The following shortlist helps you recognize how typically handle things, and offers some suggestions.

- You can memorize a piece **as you learn it**, or you can wait to memorize it once you can play it correctly.
- Memorize **small sections** at a time. For some, a small section is one or two bars; for others, it's half a page. Start with the first

section, and add subsequent sections only after you've mastered previous sections.

- Some memorize the **difficult parts** first, repeating them so often that they become as easy to play as the rest of the piece. Only after mastering the difficult parts do they include the other sections. Tip: Many teachers claim that you should never play a piece in any other order than the one intended.
- Most musicians memorize a piece from beginning to the end, but there are those who prefer to do it **the other way around**, working their way back to the beginning.
- You can also memorize bits and pieces **as you go**. Try not to look at the music while you're playing, glancing up only as you feel you need to. Bit by bit, over time, you will learn to play the entire piece by heart.
- If you **repeat a piece** or a section over and over, you're using your finger memory or tactile memory. Your fingers know what to do because they've been trained to execute the patterns that are required for that piece of music. It's a relatively easy way to memorize, but it's not very reliable. Changing the tempo of the piece may confuse you (or your fingers). If you want to know if you've really memorized the music, play it at an extremely slow tempo and see what happens.
- Alternatively, you can analyze the piece **step by step**, studying every single aspect of it. This requires a lot of knowledge (scales, harmony, etc.), but it's the most reliable way to memorize.
- Practicing a piece **away from your instrument** may help you memorize it. Just play it in your imagination, first with, then without the music. This is referred to as shadow practicing or armchair memorizing. You can also try to hear the piece in your head without playing it, before you go to sleep, or on your way to work. Or sing it while you're taking a shower.
- It also helps if you make up a **story that fits the music**!
- **Slow practicing** is good for memorizing music.

- And when you're almost done, **put the book away**. Don't leave it on the music stand, pretending or trying not to peek, but put it in the other room. Out of sight, out of mind? Then try again.

17

Being Prepared

A dry throat, butterflies in your stomach, jitters and shakes, weak knees, trembling fingers, a throbbing heart... All familiar sensations experienced by most anyone who ever climbed a stage to perform, audition, or took a music exam (and those who claim they've never experienced such symptoms are often said to be lying or dead!).

Nervousness and performing go hand in hand. It's a sign that you're undergoing an adrenaline rush, and without it, performances may be less exciting for both the players and the audience. But stage fright can get so bad that it causes you to fail an audition, not make the grade, or mess up your performance. This chapter shares some ideas on reducing audition anxiety, stage fright, and exam nerves.

Books

Many books have been written on this subject, and there is a whole lot more to be said and taught about it. The tips in this chapter touch the mere basics; and as obvious as they seem, they're often quite effective.

Adults and kids

Kids seem to suffer less from jitters and other anxiety symptoms than most teens and adults. So one of the best ways to prevent such feelings in the first place is to begin performing in public at an early age, be it with a school band, playing mini-recitals for the family every week or after each practice session — even if it's only briefly. As taking this advice may not be an option if you're already beyond early childhood, keep on reading...

PREPARING YOURSELF

First, a look at what could, or should, be done beforehand.

Practice, practice, practice

If you're not fully prepared for a performance, an audition, or a music exam, you have every reason to be nervous. Practicing efficiently, possibly under the guidance of a teacher, is one key to abating performance anxiety. A tip: The closer the time of the main event comes, the more important it is to focus practice sessions on problem areas, rather than on playing known material. A rule of thumb is to be able to play the tricky bits at least five to ten times in a row without stumbling. Only then can you be sure

that you've got them down. Tip: Make yourself start over from the beginning after each mistake, even if it's the very last note. This can make playing the final run almost as thrilling as an audition.

Too late

If you feel that you have to spend hours practicing the day before the performance, or on the actual day, you probably failed to use your previous practice sessions to the fullest.

Slips

Even professionals make mistakes, so preparing a piece includes preparing for stumbles and slips. Practice how to recover quickly and continue to play in the correct tempo. You can learn how to deal with slip-ups. One simple tip: do not make a face as this will just draw everyone's attention to your mistake. Note that there are music teachers who specialize in audition preparation!

Memory

You may play from memory to impress the jury or the members of the band, but consider bringing your sheet music along if memorization was not required. Having it there will make it easier to start over if you do slip. Does your piece require page turning? Then it would be helpful to memorize the first section on the following page. Another tip for auditions or exams: Make sure you make a list of the pieces you're going to play and bring it with you. It really doesn't look good if you've forgotten the title of your next piece.

Accompanist

If you're going to play with an accompanist during the performance, it's best if that's the person you rehearse with as well. Playing with a stranger can cause added tension, and a familiar face can be a great confidence booster. Even if not required, you may want to consider doing your piece with accompaniment (if you're not already the pianist or guitarist): Having another person there may help reduce stress, and it usually makes for a more entertaining performance too.

Deal with it

No matter how well-prepared you are, exams, auditions, and performances will induce stress and nervousness. Dealing with this is part of the learning process of playing, period. Practice doesn't make perfect, but the more you play (and the more exams or auditions you do), the better you will eventually become at handling stage fright.

Surrender

Fighting your nerves is not a good idea either. Doing so can even add to your stress level, which is probably already substantial. Telling yourself to be calm usually doesn't work either. You aren't calm, so it's actually better to just surrender to that. The fact that your nerves can make your performance less than brilliant just shows how important it is to be well-prepared.

Mock auditions

The more used to playing for an audience you are, the less likely you are to be nervous for auditions or exams. Still, these situations are different from regular performances: They occur less frequently and there's usually a lot riding on them. A mistake made during a performance typically has fewer consequences than a slip at an audition. Staging mock auditions (a.k.a. placebo auditions or dress rehearsals) often helps in getting used to the extra tension. They can take place at home, while playing for family and friends; and some teachers organize mock auditions too. Tip: Turn mock auditions into a complete performance, including a formal entrance into the room, presenting yourself, and so on. Also, ask your audience to evaluate your playing afterwards to ensure that they were attentive to every note you played. Scary? That's the idea.

Recording in advance

Recording the pieces you'll be playing at the audition or exam can by very effective. First, a recording allows you to listen and evaluate your performance, as it's very difficult to do that while you're playing. And the recorded results can give you the objectivity you need to really assess what you're doing. Second, a simple recording device can have the same effect as an attentive audience in that it can make you nervous enough to perhaps make the kind of mistakes you would in front of a real audience. Getting used to the presence of a recording device is quite similar to getting used to an audience, so that makes it effective training.

Evaluate the recording
Don't forget to evaluate the recording, and don't listen for mistakes only. Pay close attention to timing, intonation, dynamics, and all other elements that make for a great performance, including tone. Evaluating the latter requires good recording and playback equipment. Tip: First warm up, and then try to play your prepared pieces and scales right during the first take — just like in real life!

Presentation

Are you required or do you want to dress a certain way for the performance? Then decide beforehand what you're going to wear, how to wear your hair, etc. Don't wait until the day of the show to do this, but get your look together at least the day before.

Sleep
And don't forget: A good night's sleep, or a nap before an afternoon performance, often works wonders!

SHOW TIME

There are many remedies for reducing nerves on the day of your performance too. First of all, leave home early so there's no need to rush, and make sure there's plenty of time to prepare for the performance once you're on site.

Relax
For some, simply repeating the words, 'I'm calm, I'm cool,' is enough to help them relax, but most people need more than

this. There are many different techniques, ranging from deep-breathing exercises to meditation, yoga, or special methods like the Alexander Technique or neurofeedback. You may also benefit from simple stretching, jumping, and other physical movement, and for some, screaming helps.

Transfer your stress

Another idea is to find a physical release for your stress. For example, take a paperclip along and hold it when you feel nervous, imagining that all of your extra energy is being drawn through your hand into the paperclip — then throw it away before you go onstage.

Warming-up

Warm-up routines (long notes, scales, and so on) not only get you musically prepared to perform, they can also help you relax. Long, slow notes are more effective than up-tempo riffs, obviously. If you feel the need to go through your scales and prepared pieces once more, you probably aren't really ready. *Tip:* Find a quiet place to prepare, if possible.

Silence

If there's no opportunity to actually play before you go onstage, just moving your fingers over the strings of your instrument will help.

The instrument

Make sure the instrument is in good repair, and thoroughly check it before the performance. Exam judges may forgive a broken string, a failed reed, or a stuck valve, but even so, these things won't promote a confident performance. Each type of instrument requires its own specific precautions.

Tuning and warming-up

Tuning the instrument under the observant eyes of your audience, the jurors, or the examiners may be nerve-wracking, so make sure you take care of this in advance, if possible.

Imagine

Many musicians fight their nerves by conjuring calming imagery. They imagine playing at home or on their favorite stage rather

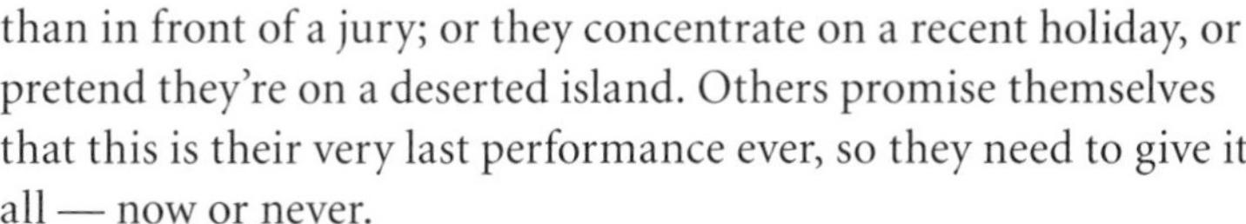

than in front of a jury; or they concentrate on a recent holiday, or pretend they're on a deserted island. Others promise themselves that this is their very last performance ever, so they need to give it all — now or never.

Pep talk

Giving yourself a pep talk may help too. But rather than just telling yourself to be cool and calm, tell yourself that you wouldn't even be here if your teacher hadn't thought you were ready — you've earned your way there.

Focus

Don't focus on the outcome of the audition or exam. Instead, concentrate on your music, as that's really what it's all about. What may also help is to make your objective the demonstration of the beauty of the music you're going to play, rather than how impressive a player you are. Final tip before going in: Smile when you enter the room. This makes you both look and feel better.

A different type of audience

Remember that auditioners and examiners are a particular kind of audience. They're there to judge your playing, rather than just enjoy the music. Still, it's good to realize that they're there for you; know that they want you to play your best and to make you feel at ease.

Any audience

It may help to calm you if you look at your examiners and auditioners the same way you'd look at a 'regular' audience: Tell yourself that they're all very kind people (which they usually are, so this shouldn't be too hard). Make eye contact with your jurors just as you would any other audience, and smile. And just as you might focus on the people you know, or the ones responding favorably to you in a regular performance, focus on the juror who smiles back at you.

The first note

Take a couple of seconds before you start playing. Breathe. Get the tempo of the piece going in your head, or even sing the first few bars in your mind; imagine yourself playing the song. Then

Imagine

Another approach is to completely ignore the audience (imagine that you're playing at home alone); but realize that this might not work at an audition or an exam. A popular method is to image the audience (large or small, jurors or not) sitting in their underwear, feeling even more uncomfortable than you are onstage. Or think of the audience as non-musicians who will be impressed by every single note you play, or as the ultimate experts who showed up just to hear you...

it's time for the first note. Make it sound great, and enjoy your performance!

AND MORE

If none of the above works for you, try consulting one of the many books on the subject. Another option is to take a yoga or meditation course, for example, or consider a drama class.

Food and drinks

Various types of food and drink are said to make anxiety worse (e.g., coffee, tea, and other products with caffeine, sugar, or salt), while others help to soothe your nerves. Bananas contain potassium, which helps you relax, and there are various types of calming herbal teas, for example.
Alcohol may make you feel more relaxed, but it definitely inhibits motor skills, judgment, and clarity — so avoid drinking alcoholic beverages.

Drugs

Many professional musicians take beta blockers (heart medication, actually) to combat their performance anxiety. This type of drug is considered relatively safe, and it works a lot faster than a yoga course and most other relaxation techniques. But you should wonder if music is your thing if you need drugs to do it, even if it's only for high-stress situations, like an audition. Try instead to reduce if not eliminate stressors; only do things that make you feel good, and avoid those that induce anxiety. Music is supposed to be fun!

Chapter 16 and 17 were taken from Tipbook Music for Kids and Teens *(see* The Tipbook Series, *page 223) and adapted for* Tipbook Violin and Viola.

Glossary

This glossary briefly explains all the jargon touched on so far. It also contains some terms that haven't been mentioned yet, but which you may come across in other books, in magazines, or online. Most terms are explained in more detail as they are introduced in this book. *Please consult the index on pages 220–222.*

Adjuster
See: *Fine tuners* and *Screw button.*

Antiquing
Technique to make violins look older than they are.

Back, back plate
The back of the body of the instrument.

Baroque violin
Special, mellow sounding gut-stringed violin, used to play the music of the Baroque era.

Bass bar
Wooden bar on the inside of the top, enhancing the lower frequencies.

Belly
See: *Top.*

Body
The body consists of a top, a back, and the sides or ribs.

Bottom nut
See: *Saddle.*

Bow
Violins and violas are played with a bow. The bow hair, attached to a slightly curved stick, makes the strings vibrate. See also: *Bow hair, Frog,* and *Stick.*

Bow grip
Piece of (synthetic) leather wrapped around the stick of the bow. Bow grip also refers to the (silver, silk or imitation baleen) *winding* or *lapping* next to it; a.k.a. *thumb grip.*

Bow hair
The hair of the bow; either horsehair or synthetic. Also know as the *ribbon.*

Bowed instruments
Instruments that are played with a bow, such as the violin, the viola, the cello and the double bass. These instruments are also indicated as 'strings'.

Bridge
The bridge transfers the vibrations of the strings to the top of the instrument.

Button
See: *End button.*

Catgut
The oldest material used for violin strings. Catgut is short for cattle gut (no cats involved!). The material used is sheep gut.

C-bout
The waist of the body.

Cello
A bowed, string(ed) instrument that sounds an octave lower than a viola.

Channel
The 'valley' near the edge of both the top and the back before the upward arching begins.

Cheeks
The sides of the pegbox.

Children's violins
See: *Fractional sizes.*

Curl
See: *Flamed wood.*

Double bass
The lowest-sounding string instrument.

Ebony
See: *Wood.*

Electric violin
An electric violin can be plugged straight into an amplifier, just like an electric guitar.

End button
The tailpiece is attached to the (end) button or *end pin.*

End pin
See: *End button.*

End screw
See: *Screw button.*

Eye
Inlaid decoration on tuning pegs, frogs, and other parts. A Parisian eye is a mother-of-pearl dot with a small metal ring around it.

***f*-hole**
The soundholes of a violin are shaped like an *f.*

Figured wood
See: *Flamed wood.*

Fine tuners
Small, additional tuning mechanisms in the tailpiece. Also referred to as *tuning adjusters, string tuners,* or *string adjusters.*

Fingerboard
When you play, you press down or *stop* the strings against the fingerboard, which is glued onto the instrument's neck.

Fittings
Collective name for the violin's replaceable parts, e.g., the tailpiece, the pegs, the nut, and even the fingerboard. The fittings are also known as the *trim.*

Flamed wood
Many violins and violas have a back and ribs which look as though they have been 'licked by flames.' This *flamed, figured,* or *curled* wood is usually more expensive than *plain wood.*

Fractional sizes
Violins and violas in small or *proportional* sizes, designed for children. Fractional-sized instruments require fractional-sized strings and fractional-sized bows.

Frog
One end of the bow hair is held in place inside the frog. At the bottom of the frog is the slide. Most frogs are *full-lined* with a metal *back plate.* At the front, where the hair enters the frog, it passes through the *ferrule* or *D-ring.*

F-stop
See: *String length.*

Full-size violin
The regular, 4/4 size violin. See also: *Fractional sizes.*

Fully-carved
Fully-carved instruments have tops and backs made by (hand) carving only.

German silver
See: *Nickel silver.*

Hair
See: *Bow hair.*

Heel
Semi-circular projection of the back.

Lining
Thin strips of wood glued to the inside edges of the body.

Luthier
Another name for a (master) violin maker.

Master violin
A violin that has been built by a master violin maker from start to finish.

Mensur ratio
See: *String length.*

Mountings
The metal parts of a bow.

Mute
A mute makes your sound a little sweeter and softer. *Practice mutes* muffle the sound a lot.

Neck
The long wooden section that extends from the instrument's body. The fingerboard is attached to the neck.

Nickel silver
Mixture of copper, zinc, and nickel (no silver!). Also known as *alpaca* and *German silver.*

Nut
The wooden strip at the top end of the neck, guiding the strings into the pegbox. Also called *top nut.*

Outfit
Violin, bow, and case.

Parisian eye
A mother-of-pearl dot with a small metal ring around it, used to decorate tuning pegs, frogs, etc.

Peg
Short for tuning peg.

Pegbox
The (tuning) pegs are fitted into the pegbox.

Peg compound, peg dope
Lubricant for tuning pegs.

Pegging
The process of fitting the tuning pegs to the instrument.

Pickup
Small, thin sensor that converts the vibrations of your strings into electrical signals.
A pickup converts an acoustic violin into an electric/acoustic instrument.

Plain strings
Unwound strings. See also: *Wound strings.*

Plain wood
See: *Flamed wood.*

Plate
1. The back and the top of the instrument. 2. Part of the bow.

Pochette
Violin with a very slim body; popular from the sixteenth well into the eighteenth century.

Practice mute
See: *Mute.*

Practice violin
A violin without a soundbox.

Proportional instruments
See: *Fractional sizes.*

Purfling
Inlaid, protective decoration around the edges of the instrument.

Quarter-cut wood, quarter-sawn wood
If you saw a tree trunk or sections of it into quarters (the way you would cut a cake into slices), you get stronger wood than if you *slab-cut* the tree.
Quarter-sawn wood allows for thin yet strong tops and backs.

Ribbon
See: *Bow hair.*

Ribs
The sides of the body.

Rosin
Used to make the bow hair sticky.

Saddle
This wooden (ebony) strip prevents the top from being damaged by the loop that holds the tailpiece in place. Also known as *bottom nut.*

Screw button
Used to tighten and relax the bow hair. Also called *end screw* or *adjuster.*

Scroll
The scroll is the head of the instrument, decorated with a *volute.* Often referred to as the *maker's signature.*

Shoulder rest
A cushion or padded support, attached to the instrument.

Sleeves
Sleeves help protect the bridge from being cut by the strings, and the strings from being damaged by the bridge.

Slide
See: *Frog.*

Sound post
Wooden rod, wedged between top and back. Often referred to as the soul of the violin.

Stick
The wooden — or synthetic — part of your bow.

Stop
See: *String length.*

Stradivarius
Antonio Stradivari, often referred to

as Stradivarius, is the world's most famous violin maker. He also built the standard model for the cello.

String adjusters
See: Fine tuners.

String height
The — adjustable — distance from the strings to the fingerboard. Also referred to as the *action.*

String length
Usually refers to the length of the strings between nut and bridge, also known as their *speaking length.* Violin makers also use the term *f*-stop, referring to the distance from the top edge of the body to the notches of the *f*-holes. The ratio between the distance from the nut to the edge, and from the edge to the notches is referred to as the *stop* or the *mensur ratio.* In violins that ratio is usually 2:3 (13:19.5 cm, equaling 5.12":7.48").
The string length is also referred to as the *scale.*

String tuners
See: *Fine tuners.*

Strings
Violin and viola strings are available in gut, synthetic-core, and steel-core versions, and with windings made of various metals. The word 'strings' is also used as a collective name for violins, violas, cellos, and double basses, a.k.a. bowed instruments.

Table
See: *Top.*

Tailgut
See: *Tailpiece, tailpiece loop.*

Tailpiece, tailpiece loop
The strings are attached to the tailpiece, and the tailpiece is attached to the end button with the tailpiece loop or *tailgut.*

Top
One of the most important components of a violin: the top of the body, also known as *table* or *belly.* The opposite side is the back.

Top nut
See: *Nut.*

Trim
See: *Fittings.*

Tuning adjusters
See: *Fine tuners.*

Tuning pegs
Violins have a tuning peg (often simply called peg) for each string. Most instruments also come with one or more fine tuners, depending on the type of strings. The peg head is known as the *thumb piece.* See also: *Fine tuners.*

Varnish
Certain varnishes may require certain cleaning methods over others. Check with a violin maker or technician.

Volute
The typically spiral-shaped decoration at the very end of the scroll.

White violins
Unfinished violins.

Winding
See: *Bow grip* and *Wound strings.*

Wolf tone, wolf tone eliminator
A wolf tone is a stuttering effect which is quite rare in violins, but common in cellos. Wolf tones can be cured using a wolf tone eliminator.

Wound strings
Strings that are wound with metal wire. Most violin and viola strings are wound strings, with the exception of the highest violin string, the E-string. This is usually an *unwound* or *plain string.*

TIPCODE LIST

The Tipcodes in this book offer easy access to short videos, sound files, and other additional information at www.tipbook.com. For your convenience, the Tipcodes in this Tipbook have been listed below.

Tipcode	Topic	Chapter	Page
VIOLIN-001	Violin and viola	1	**2**
VIOLIN-002	Various styles	1	**2**
VIOLIN-003	Stopping the strings	2	**10**
VIOLIN-004	Pizzicato	3	**20**
VIOLIN-005	Practice mute	3	**23**
VIOLIN-006	Fine tuners	5, 10	**53, 117**
VIOLIN-007	Spiccato	7	**83**
VIOLIN-008	Tuning pegs	10	**114, 122**
VIOLIN-009	Tuning fork	10	**116**
VIOLIN-010	Fifths	10	**118**
VIOLIN-011	String pitches violin	10	**120**
VIOLIN-012	String pitches viola	10	**120**
VIOLIN-013	Adjacent strings	10	**119**
VIOLIN-014	Applying rosin	11	**131**
VIOLIN-015	Removing strings	11	**134**
VIOLIN-016	Fitting strings	11	**136**
VIOLIN-017	Cello and double bass	13	**154**

Want to Know More?

Tipbooks supply you with basic information on the instrument of your choice, and everything that comes with it. Of course there's a lot more to be found on all of the subjects you came across on these pages. This section offers a selection of magazines, books, helpful websites, and organizations.

MAGAZINES

The following magazines offers tons of additional information for string players.

- *STRINGS*, www.stringsmagazine.com
- *The Strad* (UK), www.thestrad.com
- *The Journal of the Violin Society of America*, www.vsa.to (also see page 216.)
- *Journal of the American Viola Society*, www.americanviolasociety.org
- *AST Journal, Journal of the American String Teachers Association*, www.astaweb.com
- *Stringendo, Journal of the Australian Strings Association*, www.austa.asn.au
- *American Lutherie*, www.luth.org (stringed instrument making and repair; covers guitars and other fretted instruments as well)

BOOKS

There are dozens of books on violins and violas. The following is a brief selection of publications that cover some of the subjects of this Tipbook in greater depth.

- *Cambridge Companion to the Violin*, Robin Stowell (Cambridge University Press, 1993; 319 pages; ISBN 978-0521399234).
- *The Violin Explained – Components, Mechanism and Sound*, James Beament (Clarendon Press, England, 1997, 2000; 264 pages; ISBN 978-0198167396).
- *Violin and Viola*, Yehudi Menuhin and William Primrose (Kahn & Averill, 1991; 250 pages; ISBN 1871082196).
- *The Amadeus Book of the Violin: Construction, History, and Music*, by Walter Kolneder, Reinhard G. Pauly (Translator) (Amadeus Press, 1998, 2003; 602 pages; ISBN 978-1574670387).
- *Violin Owner's Manual: The Complete Guide*, Heather Scott

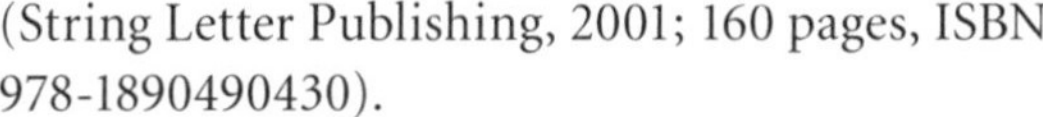

(String Letter Publishing, 2001; 160 pages, ISBN 978-1890490430).

- *History Of The Violin*, William Sandys and Simon Andrew Forster (Dover Publications, 2006; ISBN 978-0486452692).
- *Violin Repair Guide*, Michael Atria (Hal Leonard, 2004; 62 pages, ISBN 978-0634070310).
- *Violin Making: A Guide for the Amateur*, Bruce Ossman (Fox Chapel Publishing, 1998; 96 pages; ISBN 978-1565230910).

Special editions

There are also very specialized — usually quite expensive — books, often published in very limited editions, which may be of interest if you really want to go in-depth. Some examples:

- *Violin Restoration – A Manual for Violin Makers*, by Hans Weisshaar and Margaret Shipman (1988; ISBN 0962186104).
- *400 Years of Violin Making in The Netherlands* (1999; out of print).
- *The Violin Book – A Complete History* (Miller Freeman Books, 1999; limited edition).

INTERNET

There is a lot of information available online as well. Here are some websites to get you started.

- www.maestronet.com
- members.aol.com/FiddleNet
- www.viola.com (The Viola website)
- www.JazzStringCaucus.org (growth and development of string jazz and jazz education)
- www.phys.unsw.edu.au/music/violin (Violin Acoustics)
- www.digitalviolin.com
- www.violinwizard.com

- perfectfifths.com
- www.violinandviola.co.uk

Smithsonian Institution

Of course, you can also check out whether there is anything on the maker of your violin or viola by searching the Internet on that name.

If you are interested in the great old masters, take a look at The Smithsonian Institution's site at www.si.edu and search for 'violins' or 'violas'.

Looking for a teacher?

The Internet can also help you find a teacher. You may try to search for "violin teacher" or "viola teacher" and the name of the area or city where you live, consult your national string teachers association (see Associations, below), or visit one of the following special interest websites:

- PrivateLessons.com: www.privatelessons.com
- MusicStaff.com: www.musicstaff.com
- The Music Teachers List: www.teachlist.com

ASSOCIATIONS

The Violin Society Of America (VSA; 1974) promotes the art and science of making, repairing, and preserving the instruments and bows of the violin family.

The VSA organizes an annual convention that features speakers, demonstrations of instrument and bow making and repair, performances, and more. For information please visit www.vsa.to. The VSA also publishes a journal (see above) and a quarterly newsletter.

Australian Strings Association

The Australian Strings Association (www.austa.asn.au.) is a similar organization for professional and amateur instrumentalists, schools and institutions, teachers, students, conductors, and repairers and makers of string instruments.

String teachers associations

There are various associations of string teachers, such as the American String Teachers Association (www.astaweb.com) and the European String Teachers Association (www.esta-int.com). The British Branch of the European String Teachers Association can be found at www.estaweb.org.uk.

Violin makers

If you want to locate a professional violin maker, contact the American Federation of Violin and Bow Makers (www.afvbm.com); check out the Directory of Australian Violin and Bow Makers at www.abcviolins.com; or contact the British Violin Making Association (www.bvma.org.uk), for example. Similar organizations and directories can be found in other countries too.

ESSENTIAL DATA

In the event of your instrument being stolen or lost, or if you decide to sell it, it's useful to have all the relevant data at hand. Here are two pages to make those notes. For the insurance, for the police, or just for yourself. There's also room to list the strings you're currently using, for future reference.

INSURANCE

Company:

Phone: Email:

Agent:

Phone: Email:

Policy number:

Insured amount: Premium:

VIOLIN

You'll find some of the details of your violin on the label, which — if there is one at all — is usually visible through the *f*-hole on the side of the G or C-string. Some violins have labels which you can only read if the body is opened. The name of the maker can also be branded in the body, for example on the back, close to the heel.

Make and model:

Manufacturer/violin maker:

Serial number:

Color:

Make of bridge:

Tailpiece	Make:
	Type:
	Color/material:
Chin rest	Make:
	Type:
	Color/material:
Shoulder rest	Make:
	Type:
	Color/material:

Description of tuning pegs:

ANY REPAIRS, DAMAGE OR OTHER DISTINGUISHING FEATURES:

Date of purchase:	Price:
Place of purchase:	
Phone:	Email:

BOW

Make/maker:	
Type:	Price:
Octagonal/round:	Mounting:
Date of purchase:	
Place of purchase:	
Phone:	Email:

SNAREN

If you list the strings you're currently using, you'll later be able to buy the same ones if you like them, or different ones if you don't.

STRING	VIOLIN	VIOLA	MAKE	TYPE	GAUGE/TENSION	PURCHASE DATE
1:	E	A				
2:	A	D				
3:	D	G				
4:	G	C				

STRING	VIOLIN	VIOLA	MAKE	TYPE	GAUGE/TENSION	PURCHASE DATE
1:	E	A				
2:	A	D				
3:	D	G				
4:	G	C				

STRING	VIOLIN	VIOLA	MAKE	TYPE	GAUGE/TENSION	PURCHASE DATE
1:	E	A				
2:	A	D				
3:	D	G				
4:	G	C				

STRING	VIOLIN	VIOLA	MAKE	TYPE	GAUGE/TENSION	PURCHASE DATE
1:	E	A				
2:	A	D				
3:	D	G				
4:	G	C				

INDEX

Please check out the glossary on pages 205–211 for additional definitions of the terms used in this book.

S

T

V

W

THE TIPBOOK SERIES

Did you like this Tipbook? There are also Tipbooks for your fellow band or orchestra members! The Tipbook Series features various books on musical instruments, including the singing voice, in addition to Tipbook Music on Paper, Tipbook Amplifiers and Effects, *and* Tipbook Music for Kids and Teens – a Guide for Parents.

Every Tipbook is a highly accessible and easy-to-read compilation of the knowledge and expertise of numerous musicians, teachers, technicians, and other experts, written for musicians of all ages, at all levels, and in any style of music. Please check www.tipbook.com for up to date information on the Tipbook Series!

All Tipbooks come with Tipcodes that offer additional information, sound files and short movies at www.tipbook.com

Instrument Tipbooks

All instrument Tipbooks offer a wealth of highly accessible, yet well-founded information on one or more closely related instruments. The first chapters of each Tipbook explain the very basics of the instrument(s), explaining all the parts and what they do, describing what's involved in learning to play, and indicating typical instrument prices. The core chapters, addressing advanced players as well, turn you into an instant expert on the instrument. This knowledge allows you to make an informed purchase and get the most out of your instrument. Comprehensive chapters on maintenance, intonation, and tuning are also included, as well a brief section on the history, the family, and the production of the instrument.

Tipbook Acoustic Guitar

Tipbook Acoustic Guitar explains all of the elements that allow you to recognize and judge a guitar's timbre, performance, and playability, focusing on both steel-string and nylon-string instruments. There are chapters covering the various types of strings and their characteristics, and there's plenty of helpful information on changing and cleaning strings, on tuning and maintenance, and even on the care of your fingernails.

Tipbook Amplifiers and Effects – $14.95

Whether you need a guitar amp, a sound system, a multi-effects unit for a bass guitar, or a keyboard amplifier, *Tipbook Amplifiers and Effects* helps you to make a good choice. Two chapters explain general features (controls, equalizers, speakers, MIDI, etc.) and figures (watts, ohms, impedance, etc.), and further chapters cover the specifics of guitar amps, bass amps, keyboard amps, acoustic amps, and sound systems. Effects and effect units are dealt with in detail, and there are also chapters on microphones and pickups, and cables and wireless systems.

Tipbook Cello – $14.95

Cellists can find everything they need to know about their instrument in *Tipbook Cello*. The book gives you tips on how to select an instrument and choose a bow, tells you all about the various types of strings and rosins, and gives you helpful tips on the maintenance and tuning of your instrument. Basic information on electric cellos is included as well!

Tipbook Clarinet – $14.95

Tipbook Clarinet sheds light on every element of this fascinating instrument. The knowledge presented in this guide makes trying out and selecting a clarinet much easier, and it turns you into an instant expert on offset and in-line trill keys, rounded or French-style keys, and all other aspects of the instrument. Special chapters are devoted to reeds (selecting, testing, and adjusting reeds), mouthpieces and ligatures, and maintenance.

Tipbook Electric Guitar and Bass Guitar – $14.95

Electric guitars and bass guitars come in many shapes and sizes. *Tipbook Electric Guitar and Bass Guitar* explains all of their features and characteristics, from neck profiles, frets, and types of wood to different types of pickups, tuning machines, and — of course — strings. Tuning and advanced do-it-yourself intonation techniques are included.

Tipbook Drums – $14.95

A drum is a drum is a drum? Not true — and *Tipbook Drums* tells you all the ins and outs of their differences, from the type of wood to the dimensions of the shell, the shape of the bearing edge, and the drum's hardware. Special chapters discuss selecting drum sticks, drum heads, and cymbals. Tuning and muffling, two techniques a drummer must master to make the instrument sound as good as it can, are covered in detail, providing step-by-step instructions.

Tipbook Flute and Piccolo – $14.95

Flute prices range from a few hundred to fifty thousand dollars and more. *Tipbook Flute and Piccolo* tells you how workmanship, materials, and other elements make for different instruments with vastly different prices, and teaches you how to find the instrument that best suits your or your child's needs. Open-hole or closed-hole keys, a B-foot or a C-foot, split-E or donut, inline or offset G? You'll be able to answer all these questions — and more — after reading this guide.

Tipbook Keyboard and Digital Piano – $14.95

Buying a home keyboard or a digital piano may find you confronted with numerous unfamiliar terms. *Tipbook Keyboard and Digital Piano* explains all of them in a very easy-to-read fashion — from hammer action and non-weighted keys to MIDI, layers and splits, arpeggiators and sequencers, expression pedals and multi-switches, and more, including special chapters on how to judge the instrument's sound, accompaniment systems, and the various types of connections these instruments offer.

Tipbook Music for Kids and Teens – a Guide for Parents – $14.95

How do you inspire children to play music? How do you inspire them to practice? What can you do to help them select an instrument, to reduce stage fright, or to practice effectively? What can you do to make practice fun? How do you reduce sound levels and

prevent hearing damage? These and many more questions are dealt with in *Tipbook Music for Kids and Teens – a Guide for Parents and Caregivers.* The book addresses all subjects related to the musical education of children from pre-birth to pre-adulthood.

Tipbook Music on Paper – $14.95

Tipbook Music on Paper – Basic Theory offers everything you need to read and understand the language of music. The book presumes no prior understanding of theory and begins with the basics, explaining standard notation, but moves on to advanced topics such as odd time signatures and transposing music in a fashion that makes things really easy to understand.

Tipbook Piano – $14.95

Choosing a piano becomes a lot easier with the knowledge provided in *Tipbook Piano*, which makes for a better understanding of this complex, expensive instrument without going into too much detail. How to judge and compare piano keyboards and pedals, the influence of the instrument's dimensions, different types of cabinets, how to judge an instrument's timbre, the difference between laminated and solid wood soundboards, accessories, hybrid and digital pianos, and why tuning and regulation are so important: Everything is covered in this handy guide.

Tipbook Saxophone – $14.95

At first glance, all alto saxophones look alike. And all tenor saxophones do too — yet they all play and sound different from each other. *Tipbook Saxophone* discusses the instrument in detail, explaining the key system and the use of additional keys, the different types of pads, corks, and springs, mouthpieces and how they influence timbre and playability, reeds (and how to select and adjust them) and much more. Fingering charts are also included!

Tipbook Trumpet and Trombone, Flugelhorn and Cornet – $14.95

The Tipbook on brass instruments focuses on the smaller horns listed in the title. It explains all of the jargon you come across when you're out to buy or rent an instrument, from bell material to the shape of the bore, the leadpipe, valves and valve slides, and all other elements of the horn. Mouthpieces, a crucial choice for the sound and playability of all brasswinds, are covered in a separate chapter.

Tipbook Violin and Viola – $14.95

Tipbook Violin and Viola covers a wide range of subjects, ranging from an explanation of different types of tuning pegs, fine tuners, and tailpieces, to how body dimensions and the bridge may influence the instrument's timbre. Tips on trying out instruments and bows are included. Special chapters are devoted to the characteristics of different types of strings, bows, and rosins, allowing you to get the most out of your instrument.

Tipbook Vocals - The Singing Voice – $14.95

Tipbook Vocals –The Singing Voice helps you realize the full potential of your singing voice. The book, written in close collaboration with classical and non-classical singers and teachers, allows you to discover the world's most personal and precious instrument without reminding you of anatomy class. Topics include breathing and breath support, singing loudly without hurting your voice, singing in tune, the timbre of your voice, articulation, registers and ranges, memorizing lyrics, and more. The main purpose of the chapter on voice care is to prevent problems.

International editions

The Tipbook Series is also available in Spanish, French, German, Dutch, Italian, Swedish, and Chinese. For more information, please visit us at www.tipbook.com.

TIPBOOK SERIES MUSIC AND MUSICAL INSTRUMENTS

Tipbook Acoustic Guitar
ISBN 978-1-4234-6523-2, HL00332802 – $14.95

Tipbook Amplifiers and Effects
ISBN 978-1-4234-6277-4, HL00332776 – $14.95

Tipbook Cello
ISBN 978-1-4234-5623-0, HL00331904 – $14.95

Tipbook Clarinet
ISBN 978-1-4234-6524-9, HL00332803 – $14.95

Tipbook Drums
ISBN 978-90-8767-102-0, HL00331474 – $14.95

Tipbook Electric Guitar and Bass Guitar
ISBN 978-1-4234-4274-5, HL00332372 – $14.95

Tipbook Flute & Piccolo
ISBN 978-1-4234-6525-6, HL00332804 – $14.95

Tipbook Home Keyboard and Digital Piano
ISBN 978-1-4234-4277-6, HL00332375 – $14.95

Tipbook Music for Kids and Teens
ISBN 978-1-4234-6526-3, HL00332805 – $14.95

Tipbook Music on Paper – Basic Theory
ISBN 978-1-4234-6529-4, HL00332807 – $14.95

Tipbook Piano
ISBN 978-1-4234-6278-1, HL00332777 – $14.95

Tipbook Saxophone
ISBN 978-90-8767-101-3, HL00331475 – $14.95

Tipbook Trumpet and Trombone, Flugelhorn and Cornet
ISBN 978-1-4234-6527-0, HL00332806 – $14.95

Tipbook Violin and Viola
ISBN 978-1-4234-4276-9, HL00332374 – $14.95

Tipbook Vocals – The Singing Voice
ISBN 978-1-4234-5622-3, HL00331949 – $14.95

Check www.tipbook.com for additional information!